OUR STORIES

things we know now we wish we knew then

National Alliance on Mental Illness
NAMI San Fernando Valley

Library of Congress Control Number 2011962712
CreateSpace, North Charleston, SC

Our Stories
Things We Know Now We Wish We Knew Then /San Fernando, NAMI

Published in the United States by
National Alliance on Mental Illness (NAMI) San Fernando Valley
14545 Sherman Circle, Van Nuys, CA 91405
www.namisfv.org

ISBN: 1468001485
ISBN-13: 978-1468001488

CONTENTS

DEDICATION

Our Stories, *Things We Know Now, We Wish We Knew Before* is dedicated to the courageous and creative San Fernando Valley family members who first stood up to the stigma of mental illness in 1975 to establish what was to become the National Alliance on Mental Illness.

Our Stories, *Things We Know Now, We Wish We Knew Before* is also dedicated to all the families and individuals who have followed in their footsteps and to our 2011 NAMI SFV leaders instrumental in bringing this project to fruition.

WHAT NAMI SFV MEANS TO ME ...

"I am deeply indebted to NAMI and a number of its members for tremendous amounts of support and care."

"We share our NAMI experience to help educate those around us about mental illness and to help reduce the stigma associated with this disease that touches so many families."

"It is rewarding and comforting to be involved with others who truly understand."

"This book will serve many, many people. Thank you for the opportunity to help."

"I'm grateful to be a member of NAMI-SFV; it has become a part of why I'm in a strong state of recovery."

"NAMI gave my family strength and support for one another. I can't say enough about the wonderful people that guided my family to where they are today."

ABOUT NAMI SFV

NAMI SFV, National Alliance on Mental Illness, San Fernando Valley is an all-volunteer grassroots organization. Our programs and services are offered in English and Spanish and are free to those in need of help and support, including classes, presentations, support groups, lending library, online resources, and more throughout the San Fernando and Santa Clarita Valleys in Los Angeles County.

NAMI SFV is proud to have been the foundation of a national organization that has grown to include affiliates in all 50 states, Puerto Rico and Guam. To find the NAMI affiliate closest to you, visit www.nami.org

OUR MISSION

The mission of NAMI SFV, National Alliance on Mental Illness, San Fernando Valley, is to improve the lives of those affected by severe mental illness. We provide advocacy, awareness, education, resources, and support for individuals and families whose lives are touched by mental illness. We encourage you to contact us or visit our website for information on our programs and services.

Visit us online
www.namisfv.org

NAMI SFV
BOARD OF DIRECTORS 2011

JOE CONRAD, President

DAVID STAIRS, Secretary

BARBARA GAUTHIER, Treasurer

BETH ARNOLD, 1st Vice President

MILTON DECKER, 2nd Vice President

JULIA ROBINSON SHIMIZU, 3rd Vice President

ZEE DANKWORTH

MARY HARPEL

AL HENRIQUEZ

DANIEL MAHONEY

JIM RANDALL

SUZANNE SCHMITDKE

TOM WALSH

LETTER FROM THE PRESIDENT

My name is Joe Conrad and I am the current President of NAMI San Fernando Valley Affiliate, NAMI SFV. I want to share with you how this project came to be and how I first got involved. I do this as a way to provide some insight into what NAMI affiliates do and encourage you to become involved at some level wherever you may live. NAMI SFV was approached by Wisdom Legacy's founder, Dave Burrill at one of our Special Projects Committee meetings. Special Projects is an incubation group that NAMI SFV uses to nurture ideas and attract volunteers. In fact, it is how I got involved with our affiliate. I was looking for a way to give back when I was invited to attend a Special Projects meeting. The rest, as they say, is history.

When I heard this would become a published book and would contribute to a web-based database for family members and their loved ones, I was hooked. I strongly believe the Wisdom Legacy concept of "If I knew then, what I know now, what would I do differently" offers a meaningful store of wisdom as well as an opportunity for NAMI families to put our experience to good use. The contents of this book will help others facing similar life challenges. I agreed to see this project through to fruition and am so proud to present it to you now. The stories in this book have been written by over 50 NAMI SFV authors.

My own journey began when one of our sons was exhibiting behavior well outside the norm. After several hospitalizations, arrests and "special schools" it was apparent that we needed help. "If I knew then, what I know now…" I would have dealt with the impact of our son's situation differently. My wife attended a NAMI Family to Family class. I checked out Al Anon and attended a NAMI Special Projects meeting. Soon, I was asked to take over the Committee, then a board position was offered. The following year, I became President. I am glad to help our affiliate expand to offer more of our signature programs to our diverse community.

Living in Los Angeles, I am a die-hard LA Lakers basketball fan. After they won a 16th championship in 2010, I was wearing my good luck Ron Artest (now Metta World Peace) #37 replica team jersey when I heard Mr. Artest interviewed on TV. The first words out of his mouth were, "First, I want to thank my psychologist" I thought, 'Wow. He might be able to help us promote our book and make it more visible.' After months of wading through a sea of representatives, I made contact with "his people" and Mr. Artest graciously agreed to write the foreword for this book.

I want to thank everyone who participated in helping me get this book to you. First of all, Lorna Boyd was instrumental in helping our authors gain access, troubleshoot issues and promote participation. Lynn Conrad (yep, my wife) supported me and helped with editing the book along with Valeria Reyes and Lorna Boyd. A big thanks goes to Rita Keeley Brown, who is in her own right a published author, for editing. I want to thank all of our board members for their support, encouragement and participation and particularly Julia Robinson Shimizu for editorial leadership and Ichiro Shimizu for cover design.

I am exceptionally proud of the honesty and candor of **Our Stories**. Thank you for taking up this book, I believe you will benefit from our NAMI SFV Wisdom Legacy.

Joe Conrad

President, NAMI SFV

ABOUT WISDOM LEGACY

Wisdom Legacy was conceived in 2002 to capture and record one million stories about life's most important lessons from people who have 'been there.' The idea was to use the wisdom conveyed in these stories to create an on-line encyclopedia of lessons. We were fortunate to have a member of the prestigious Board of Editors of the Encyclopedia Britannica to guide us through the process.

The final group who helped us looked like a small army of PhDs. The team included psychologists, pastors, cultural anthropologists, educators, authors, business executives, entrepreneurs, and board members of publicly traded companies, doctors, nurses and public health officials, current and past top-level government officials including two who had reported directly to Presidents Carter and Reagan, a former Surgeon General of the Navy, management consultants, attorneys, executives, software experts, scientists, engineers, journalists, artists, athletes, musicians, and experts on gerontology, addictions, trauma and abuse. This incredible team volunteered over 30,000 hours.

The resulting Wisdom Legacy website includes customized questions for specific life experiences, a library to organize lessons learned, and a search engine to quickly locate specific content. Wisdom Legacy proves there are answers to your questions, and people out there to help you find them.

All my best,

David P. Burrill
Chief Executive Officer, Wisdom Legacy

WISDOM LEGACY MISSION

Wisdom Legacy allows individuals, families and friends to record their most important experiences to harvest the wisdom that comes from wrestling with life's challenges. Our goal is to compile lessons about what works from one million people, and use that knowledge to mentor future generations.

Our hope is to advance the emotional and spiritual health of our community not only to celebrate life, but to lend support and compassion to those who find themselves heartbroken or isolated.

We also want to share with them the hope and joy that comes from knowing that we are not alone, our challenges are not unique, solutions do exist, and all of us have both the opportunity and capability to thrive.

Wisdom Legacy engages people in dialogue about the important stuff of life and serves those seeking growth, wisdom and understanding.

What do you know today
that you wish you had known before?

Please, tell us your story at
www.WisdomLegacy.org

FOREWORD

There are more important things in life than winning the world championship. For me, fighting and winning the battle for mental health and recovery has proven to be the most difficult and most important thing. I never imagined when I was a kid growing up in New York that I would have so much or that I would be so close to losing it all. I am a basketball player and I am good at it, but I became an advocate for mental health when I realized that I risked losing everything if I could not control my mental health. Sure, I was called crazy for things I did, and that's not uncommon. What is unusual is that I dared to talk about my struggles with my mental health when I acknowledged my psychologist after winning the championship. Some people thought that was crazy, some thought that as a champion athlete, admitting a weakness was crazy. But I realized that there is no health without mental health and I came to understand and respect the value of getting help and overcoming stigma. I realized I could help others get the help they need by simply talking about my struggles. I love being a winner and I love the applause when my team wins a game, but I think there are far more important things in this world and I applaud NAMI, The National Alliance on Mental Illness, for helping families and individuals understand mental illness, for helping people achieve mental health, and for all they do to overcome the stigma attached to mental illness. I am honored to lend my name to this important book that I am certain will help so many people. Read it in good health!

Ron Artest

Metta World Peace
Los Angeles Lakers

WELCOME TO OUR STORIES NAMI SFV WISDOM LEGACY

The lives of each of the individuals who contributed to this project have been touched by severe mental illness. For many of us, finding NAMI, The National Alliance on Mental Illness, was an important step in taking control of our lives with awareness, education and action.

The whirlwind of upheaval and uncertainty at the onset of mental illness demands a new perspective. Mental Illness created a divide in our lives, a before and after: before we recognized the symptoms, before we knew what to do, before we understood what was happening, before we found help and guidance, comfort, community and solace in NAMI; and after we had a diagnosis, after we came to terms with the realities of living with a brain disorder, after we began to master the tools of recovery or survival, after we found a new sense of hope, after we began to accept and explore this new path our lives had taken.

The Wisdom Legacy project has provided our NAMI affiliate an opportunity to share with the world some measure of our accomplishment. With the tragedies and turmoil inherent in living with severe mental illness, be it mental illness in a family member, a friend or ourselves, we have all learned valuable lessons. Wisdom Legacy allows us to share Our Stories, what we learned along the way, with others who may benefit.

As you read this collection of life experiences, you may see yourself or your loved one reflected in the stories. They are presented by topic, as answers to questions, so no one story is told all the way through, and there are snippets that may seem to jump around, as from "my son" to "my children," or "he" to "she," etc.

If we have done what we set out to do, you may learn from these experiences and be helped by them, recognizing that you are not the only one, that others have "been there, done that" and can offer encouragement and hope, and some very practical solutions.

We encourage you to share these very personal stories. Some are heartbreaking, some are humorous, some show us as we stumble in our attempt to do the right thing, some resonate with hope, some sing with possibility. All of Our Stories are heartfelt offerings of the wisdom we gained as we traveled this unexpected path.

YOUR CHILD & MENTAL ILLNESS

A child's mental illness deeply affects a family's life.

What initially made you think your child might be mentally ill and when did this happen?

He was a very easy child, honor student, very smart and kind. Then missing school, bad grades, rude behavior, dishonesty... Taking drugs, drinking. New friends. He finally admitted not feeling well, but refused to see a doctor. But by this time he was eighteen, and I was not allowed to make an appointment.

⚜

As a teenager, my son was very withdrawn, mostly in public settings. He did have many friends in the apartment complex where we lived. In school, although he was in baseball, he didn't hang around the other players. He did not participate in any of the after-game gatherings. He did not want to participate in family functions. He would still attend church services, but would not make eye contact with anyone and would sit huddled in a ball. His delusional outbursts continued. Finally, we took him to see a therapist and he was diagnosed with social phobia, bipolar, and schizoaffective disorder. He was on many different medications, but to no avail.

From the start my two children, who are now diagnosed, exhibited odd behaviors starting as early as age two or so. They were violent to domestic animals and insects. They would talk to themselves in the third person. My children would do odd finger movements over and over again and pull out their eyelashes or pinch their skin on their hands till they bled.

I always knew there was something unique about my children; I just did not know what it was. As a mother that 'gut instinct' was right on. I was not familiar with child-hood psychosis or childhood bipolar, so although I knew it was not normal for my children to exihibit such behaviors or habits, I had no clue how serious it was.

I remember the time when he was about five or six and something fairly innocuous happened. He was wearing *Ninja Turtle* roller skates and was on his back, kicking and screaming out of control. Other times, he'd react without the slightest provocation. I couldn't tell if he were serious or not. We felt bad for him and his two brothers whenever this took place. They both labeled him as an 'idiot, jerk, negative force,' which, of course, he took to heart. This became his identity, and maybe was the beginning of the self-hatred. Later on, he would refer to himself as "Dark" so he realized what was going on, at some level.

2

My son changed gradually changed from being an honor student and very well liked. His grades were dropping, he started to lie, was absent from school, and rude to others. When he was 18 it was very clear, that something was very wrong.

It seems like K was always different. Even as a toddler, she couldn't get along well with other children. She would always fight with them. I would meet the parents of a little girl she had just made friends with and began to see a pattern, that this would be the last time she would get along with her and they became enemies. She would have "secret friends" – girls who would play with her in private and would not admit to being friends.

As a young child, K could not stop moving. She needed constant stimulation and had to be the center of attention. She was unable to interact peacefully and unable to share with other children. K would sometimes have a mean side to her—she would say or do whatever she had to in order to gain others' attention. She also masturbated from a very early age. She would rub her bottom against surfaces and she would do it anywhere and at any time.

We enrolled her in a Montessori preschool, and she was kicked out because she accused the teachers of hitting her and would not do projects the way that the teachers instructed the kids to do them.

My "problem" child is my son .... who is now in his early forties. I never actually thought he had a mental illness and am still not sure. I do know that, in retrospect, there were some issues that stand out from his teens: shyness, difficulty sleeping at night, anxiety, and then alcohol abuse, which I believe started after a period of pot use. He later became an alcoholic, probably starting during freshman year in college, but it took us (my husband and me) a long time to come to grips with it. We were not helped in any great measure by college administration that seemed determined to protect him. They threatened him with suspension, but never acted on it.

There was a change in behavior in senior year of high school for my son. He withdrew socially from activities, wanted to change high schools, persuaded us that he wanted to join the Navy and became isolated. We sent him to a psychologist who told us after several sessions that he needed medications and a psychiatrist.

When our daughter was nine and a half she started showing signs of OCD. It became very obvious over the course of several months, as she would wash her hands up to thirty times a day, which left her knuckles cracked and bleeding. She would also refuse to touch her clothing for fear that they were contaminated by someone with AIDS or that she may have accidentally come in contact with Oleander (a plant that is deadly if eaten but grows everywhere in the community).

We tried Behavioral Therapy, which did not work and started her on Prozac which worked wonders. At age eleven she began cutting, or self-mutilating. At first she would do it in response for not getting her way. It was her way of lashing out. Over the course of the next four years she would battle cutting along with depression and anxiety. It was not until after she took her life at fifteen and a half that her psychiatrist said he would have diagnosed her not just as suffering from depression and anxiety, but as bipolar. He also believed that at the time she made the decision to end her life, she was having a psychotic episode.

My son was having trouble in college. He was failing and was drinking excessively. He came home and started to tell me he noticed his head was always spinning and he could not control his thoughts. After taking him to several doctors, we found out he had Obsessive Compulsive Disorder (OCD), obsessing on thoughts. At that time I learned of NAMI. Thank goodness.

I am not a medical doctor nor a psychiatrist, but I am the parent of a boy who has had a very difficult life. I've loved him unconditionally since the day we adopted him at birth, from a methamphetamine-addicted birth mother and an unknown father. I have protected him, made excuses for his behavior, hand-picked his education, taken him to some of the best doctors, tried alternative treatments, medication trials, residential treatment, mental hospitals, wilderness training and on and on. I fit the criteria for being the classic enabler, and boy, was I good at it – not that I'm proud.

I have watched him go from a beautiful, cuddly baby, to a teen who wouldn't let anyone touch him. I watched as he began to have uncontrollable rages, violent oubursts, interest in witchcraft and the occult. I live with him and love him, even while he terrorized his younger brother, pushed his father down a flight of stairs, threatened the family with weapons, and stopped going to school.

The police came to know us well, as we often had to rely on them for help. The drywall workers were kept busy patching the holes in doors and walls created by our son's feet, fists, and thrown objects. The neighbors started being afraid when they found our son in their homes uninvited. They started locking their doors. We got used to keeping our windows closed, hoping to prevent the world from knowing what we were going through.

I never left my younger son alone with his brother and was always at the ready to protect my younger child from my older, both physically and emotionally. We hired behaviorists, enrolled him in therapy and social skills groups. We took parenting classes, went through group, family, and individual counseling and eventually couples therapy. We went from worrying for our son, who didn't choose his disabilities, to worrying about the safety of our lives. We had become afraid for our son – and afraid of him.

Our son was eighteen and had just gone away to college when he became ill. Until that time, we thought it was just teenage trouble, but his breakdown at college made it clear there was something very, very wrong. Now that we know more about the progression of mental illness, we might have taken early symptoms more seriously. Signs of depression, confusion and 'poverty of speech' were there, the social isolation had already begun; but we didn't recognize them as symptoms of mental illness. We imagined he was simply being difficult, withdrawing from us.

We couldn't have been expected to know, but if we had, we might have spent those early years working harder to understand his needs and get him help.

She was always a very happy, easy going child. However, shortly after our family became deeply involved in the care of my sister-in-law who was terminally ill, she began to change. At first we thought it was just teenage stuff' and that she was withdrawing due to the stress of the family situation at the time. However, when it became clear that she really was not ok she actually was able to tell us what was wrong.

She began to describe how she was feeling, using words and phrases that I use to describe my clinical depression – numbness, loss of interest in things that used to delight her, feeling like she was seeing the world through gauze, and so on. And then it became clear that she also had clinical depression which she came by genetically through me. She was about fifteen at the time and has been on Wellbutrin ever since, learning to live with her disease.

⚜

The first clue that something was 'off' about my son was the four-hour temper tantrums by the age of one. Temper tantrums consisting of screaming and crying until his face turned purple and he was hyperventilating. That was for being told "No" or taking something away he wanted.

Those temper tantrums progressed to include bashing his head against the floor or sidewalk by the age of two. Next thing that seemed odd was that, after almost twelve hours of running and playing in daycare, he would still be so hyper that it would take two hours to get him to calm down in order to eat. Then, he couldn't sleep. He would be awake until midnight, have nightmares or report seeing skeletons, bloody and gory things and then be back up again.

It only got worse when he started school. He would be very hyper and distracted even in kindergarten. Then he would come home and be so stressed that his temper tantrums became more violent, he would attempt to harm himself and he was scared of everything. The school suspected he may have ADHD and recommended that he be put on medicine. We tried it and it calmed and focused him a little but he was still very angry and hyper all the time. By age six, he was hospitalized for psychosis due to his chronic nightmares and visions, continued violence toward himself and others, and his inability to eat due to stress/hyperactivity. Diagnosis: bipolar disorder.

How has your child's condition impacted the way you parent?

Denial is a poisonous word for a parent of a mentally ill child. I could see that my child was behaving differently than other children. I could read the signs because I myself am bipolar. At first, I didn't want to believe that somehow he could have hit this unfortunate genetic lottery and acquired my affliction. I made a lot of excuses for him from the way he acted to the things he said. My life was spent in quiet despair. I was so sad that my child, then 5 years old, needed real help. Although his teachers agreed with me that he needed more serious help than was the norm, they were reluctant to indicate any form of mental illness. They just said, "He's naughty and needs more discipline". Somehow, it was my parenting that was at fault causing him to be in such turmoil. I went through all of the proper school channels and didn't receive much help.

In the second grade, they tested him as highly gifted and told me that his genius was causing him to be difficult. I knew I was in this alone. As a parent, I had to be my child's biggest advocate. You know that saying, "If you want something done right, do it yourself." Well, that's a partial truth. You certainly have to jump-start it. I investigated all options and managed to push for a one-on-one in his classroom.

I always thought being a mom meant soccer practice and PTA meetings. Soccer was a nightmare and the PTA meetings were usually about how to get my child out of the 'regular' classroom.

By age fifteen, my son had a major depressive episode and stayed in bed for almost a year. He was awake for maybe two hours a day and all two hours were filled with violent outbursts (and he was a very big boy by this time). I had to lock my door at night. He was failing in school and the school was threatening to have me arrested for child endangerment because I was allowing him to stay in bed. There were some hospitalizations during that time but he was not getting better. My mama-bear claws came out and I fought. I woke up one day and decided to grab hold of any resources I possibly could that would benefit my son. He was drowning in school. I waited at UCLA to have him tested three times. I knocked on doors of doctors, lawyers, teachers, and social workers. I threaded my son through the system and used it like a net to cradle him to a safe place. I guard that net to this day and my son is almost twenty-one. I home-schooled him and he graduated high school with his diploma on time.

I would see other parents at the park having picnics with their kids or coaching their basketball teams and I knew that wouldn't happen for me. However, today, when I get a big hug from my six-foot tall, sweet boy who has come such a long way and he says, "You are the best mom in the whole world. Thanks for everything. I love you!" I know I've done the right things.

I know we are hardly through this and any day can bring on something new... but I cherish the "I love you, Mom" moments and they re-play in my head and it gets me through the rough patches.

⚜

Our child's mental illness has deeply affected our life. The lives of all of our family members have been forever changed from our daughter's illness. Our sense of security and confidence in having a good life and being happy has been woefully undermined. Mental illness had never been something that we ever considered as a threat. I guess we never thought it could happen to us. Now we see that even with everything on your side, psychosis can still sideline anyone, and not just the person with the problem, but the whole family. Having said that, I think we've all come out of it stronger, but as a mother I can't help wondering how things "might have been" had this not happened to us.

How did you come to get a diagnosis for your child? What was that diagnosis?

Our family went through a traumatic and devastating divorce after twenty years, and my teenage son showed signs of depression and extreme anxiety about attending school. After much difficulty and chaos, he was hospitalized initially for two weeks. It was a scary experience for him, and because of my lack of knowledge and my own devastation, I was unable to do more for him at the time.

He continued to decline and ultimately had a very serious psychotic episode and ended up in the hospital for four months. There were family meetings there, but I don't recall any real education from the doctors or staff about my son's chronic illness. His diagnosis at that time was manic-depressive disorder. I had a big brother who had this same diagnosis and seemed very high functioning and normal most of the time. He even ran a business, was married and took medication.

I don't think I grasped at all the longevity of the illness, and certainly was not given any instructions on what to expect. I don't think my son was initially given much information either initially on how to manage his illness. He was released to his father, who couldn't keep him and brought him to me. I don't remember being given a treatment plan or support guidance. There was no real follow up plan that I remember.

Next he began to get into trouble, experimenting with drugs and hanging with the wrong friends. Thus began the long journey of his very difficult and challenging life in many facilities; jail, Board-and-Care, etc. A very long saga of ups and downs, very few successful periods. This son is now in his 40's and still is very challenged with maintaining sobriety and stability. I am very grateful to have found NAMI. My involvement has made me feel understood, 'not so alone,' and has helped me learn some better ways of coping, and helped me meet people who can direct me to better resources and better help. And it keeps me from losing hope.

It wasn't until parents of children on my daughter's soccer team told me that they thought she was ADHD, that I began to realize that there was a possible diagnosis. I didn't have insurance, so I took her to a general practice doctor who agreed with what the parents had said, and gave her Ritalin. I saw a great improvement. When I finally got her into the AB 3632 program, the diagnosis was confirmed again. After her first bipolar episode, she was hospitalized and was diagnosed bipolar and ADHD.

⚜

We were told he was suffering from schizophrenia. However, UCLA doctors always said he was an enigma. Perhaps drugs triggered the first onset, but this is not a typical case.

What have been the barriers and successes in working with healthcare professionals to help your child?

It was tough not having insurance when we needed services for K. I had always had her in private schools because the schools in our neighborhood were not very good. No one told me that K could have had Los Angeles Unified School District (LAUSD) services even in private school, or even that they had services. Fortunately, I got a job at UCLA and was able to transfer her to Fairview, a public school close by for her last year in elementary school. The principal went out of her way to advocate for K to get services through AB3632. That was when K had her first testing and IEP.

It was so great to have support finally. She was able to get into a program at Hathaway, which at that time was in Lakeview Terrace, and had a therapist and psychiatrist. We met as a family with the therapist as well. She also had someone who came to the school and assisted her with socialization.

K enrolled in schools with Magnet Programs in middle school, first at Madison, then at Pacoima. She thrived during that time. She decided to go to Van Nuys High School's Magnet Program. Unfortunately, the school is very large, and for the first time, she didn't get the support she needed, and she had her first manic episode after a couple of months at Van Nuys.

She ended up in the hospital and they gave her the diagnosis of Bipolar. While she was in the hospital, we had an IEP and it was decided that K needed to be in a non-public school environment. So she went to North Hills Prep, and she did well and graduated from there.

We were able to get K on Medi-Cal and eventually she got SSI/SSDI services. She did well until they would no longer allow her to get Zyprexa. The doctors tried other meds and K ended up very unstable and was in the hospital four to five times in a year.

During that time, I joined NAMI and took the Family to Family classes. Through the contacts I made, I got a referral to someone in the Department of Mental Health that referred her to the Full Service Partnership (FSP) program at Cornerstone. That saved her! The psychiatrist advocated for K and got her back on Zyprexa and her case workers helped her get back into community college, and moving toward a career. They also assisted her in becoming independent again, and into less restrictive housing (she had been at a Board-and-Care, and moved into what is called an SRO, which is more of a rooming house. She is now about to rent a room in a house. I don't think she would be doing as well as she is without the great support from the FSP program.

Sadly, it seems that many professionals have excluded the family from involvement with their loved ones. Especially when that loved one becomes an adult. Many professionals seem only to have book knowledge of disorders and do not seem to realize that family members can give more accurate information than the client. I would hope that professionals would be required to get accurate information from the families and not be restricted in gaining information that could be helpful with diagnosis and recovery for clients with serious mental illnesses.

NAMI has helped me learn that I am not restricted from providing information to the doctors or staff that might be trying to help my loved one. They may discount that information if they are not instructed to value it, and see that it can be very helpful. NAMI's work with stigma and advocacy has helped providers of services to be more open, and so communication with families has improved. However, continued education efforts and advocacy is extremely important.

I have been successful in better advocacy for my loved one by making sure that I know and have an opportunity to talk with the social services provider or case manager for my loved one. If I mention that I am a member of the National Alliance on Mental Illness, or ask if they are aware of that organization, they hopefully talk more openly with me. I can provide information to them about NAMI and suggest they check the website, and that this support and advocacy organization has been in existence well over thirty years. In NAMI, I have learned how to communicate better with the professionals regarding my loved one.

What have you experienced with this child that has changed your relationships with your other children or family members?

In the course of the years that we have been dealing with my son's alcoholism and many times untreated depression, either as a result of sobriety or a precursor to the drinking, we found ourselves focusing way too much on his well-being to the detriment of our younger daughter. She honestly has always been a terrific kid, smart and independent, and seemingly able to manage on her own much better than could really be expected. At some point, actually not too many years ago, she confronted us and asked us not to talk about her brother when we spoke to her on the phone (both her brother and she live in another state). It was difficult. Bad habits are hard to break, but we tried and eventually became pretty good at it.

This seemed to coincide with a time when we actually started to let go of trying to control his problems for him. Our being able to let go also seemed to help her and her husband look at her brother with greater understanding. They are now able to stay in contact with him and socialize with him when he is sober, and stay away from him when he is bingeing.

As I am sure many family members recognize my husband and I, on the whole, manage our lives better now. But we honestly, always feel only as well as our least-well child, and most of the time, that is our son. At the present time, he has not done well over the last three years, and it is hard to deal with.

He has young children for whom he is responsible most of the time, and that, of course, has introduced a whole other dimension into the dynamic. The mother of the children is as selfish as he is and does not provide much, if any, stability in the kids' lives. In fact, it is weird that our son seems to be the better parent, especially, of course, during his periods of sobriety. These currently seem to last two, three to four months, then there is another binge.

How did you feel after reality sunk in?

At loss, how to deal with it emotionally. Anxiety.

It sounds stupid now, but I remember feeling relieved to finally have an actual name put to what was wrong, what we had been going through with my bipolar son. Of course we cried. And it was hard to see (or *feel*) the reaction of friends to his diagnosis—back in 1999, bipolar disorder wasn't quite so "popular" as it is now. If people only knew that throwing that term around so casually is inappropriate and hurtful to those who know its pain. I looked around for someone to blame, some explanation, some reason this could possibly be happening to my perfectly normal and beautiful family.

I read every book I could find, but nothing prepared me for the complex feelings that come with accepting mental illness as a part of our life. It was here, and it came to stay. Never mind the long periods of seeming normality when my son was able to convince the world that he was brilliant and happy. Lurking under every expression, every beautiful smile, winsome gesture, and proud achievement was this illness eating away at his sanity, until he couldn't stand it any longer. The reality of his death was the final blow. It all seems like a fog now, a distant, unfathomable fog that took my boy away from me and the world. And I feel like we never saw it coming, even though we knew he was sick.

I wish I had understood more about how individually mental illness strikes, looking different on different people, and how insidious it is. I have since learned a lot from NAMI that might have helped me, but I didn't make that connection back then, and no one ever suggested it. I hope this book will help direct people towards the great support that is out there.

What's the hardest part of your day?

When I am at home. My son and husband despise each other and do not talk. There is a lot of tension in the air and my son refuses help of any kind. He spends most of the time in his room sleeping, and stays up during the night doing his laundry.

How do you deal with the stress that a mentally ill child places on a marriage?

It changes everything, it has been a total nightmare. The things you do trying to keep things and yourself functioning, working, maintaining everyday responsibilities. Keeping a normal image, keeping your painful secrets to yourself.

Ours is a somewhat challenging situation in that I, the mother, live with clinical depression, my older daughter has depression and my younger daughter has an anxiety disorder. My husband has none of this. So it has been a life of educating him as to the specifics of both disorders and helping him to better understand what each of us is going through and how he can, and cannot, help us. And then it takes a lot of patience to deal with my children's issues, especially when I can sense that my own depression is overwhelming me.

All in all we try to take things slowly and remind one another as to the specifics of each disorder and to remember that the tensions come from the illness, not each of us. We try to ride out each bout of depression or anxiety.

❧

Disciplining our children has become a tug of war between my husband and me. Although my children are diagnosed with a mental illess, I still try to instill in them the same values and beliefs as I have for my children who hold no diagnoses. My husband has stated "you're being too mean or too strict. He's not like the others. They don't understand like the other kids."

My belief is that indeed they are like the others and they will show respect, not be a danger to themselves or others, follow rules, be honest and play nice as expected from my other children. It has caused me stress, and has had a toll on the marriage. It has also made me question my expectations from my sons, and made me question, "Am I being a fair mommy to these children?"

❧

Our son's illness has been a great gift to our marriage. We are united in ways we had never imagined. We draw strength from one another. We offer patience and kindness to one another that may not have come to us in any other way.

In the beginning, we felt very much alone. We are fortunate to have turned to one another. NAMI helped us do that. We know this could just as easily have ripped us apart. We rarely agreed on anything related to raising our son before he became ill, and we still disagree. But we have learned so much through NAMI, and particularly through NAMI Family to Family class, that we are able to cope, together.

It sounds silly to anyone who has not been through this, but we even remind each other about passages in the NAMI Family to Family class. Communication. Loss. Grief. Coping. We have learned how to hope in a different way. Most important, we have learned how to cope in a more graceful way.

It is as if our son's illness is a fire-breathing dragon. We have gathered our forces against this magnificent monster and are able to stand strong, unified in battle. Side by side. Day by day. Year after year. We need and appreciate each other more as we battle forward towards our son's potential recovery or at least towards some sort of peace. And we do it together.

How do you address the basic issues of parenting—nurture, discipline, expectations, babysitting, and education— within the context of your child's condition?

Being a parent to a child with early onset Bipolar teaches you more about yourself and keeping faith in your child. However you may have been parented must be relearned and applied individually to your child. Read about the illness, the effects on behavior, go to therapy for yourself, and participate with your child's therapist as much as possible. Forgiveness of yourself and your child is foremost in learning to nurture. Forgiveness for your faults so you don't mistake nurture for guilt and forgiveness of the child's behavior so you will remember to not take his/her behavior personally and therefore will continue to show him/her that they are loved.

Discipline – throw out both extremes of mythology regarding discipline. Being too harsh won't change who they are and being too soft just gives them room to manipulate. They are experts at manipulation. Consistency and established but flexible rules become the way. They need to know you mean it when you say no (or yes) and what you expect their behavior to be. Then we move on to expectations. That one is hardest. As a parent you battle with the notion of what a normal child is capable of versus 'this' child. Learn to trust, not blame, your child's recognition of his/her limitations. What may look like laziness or defiance may actually be lack of understanding or coordination or they may be just too stressed right then to perform. That is why rules must be consistent and flexible. As the parent, you need to slow down, take smaller steps and be calm. Your child wants to reach your expectations of them, just don't set them so high that they will fail. The same goes for yourself. You are not Superman or Wonder Woman. You will feel as if you failed them and just as you forgive them for their shortcomings, you must forgive yourself.

Was the realization that you were dealing with mental illness sudden and traumatic or a slow evolution?

Our introduction to our daughter's mental illness was sudden and brutally traumatic. She had her first psychotic break when we were spending a long weekend in Yosemite National Park. We were renting a condo and had been out sightseeing most of the day and returned to the condo where we played games in the evening, a perfectly normal day for us. Our daughter and her boyfriend were evidently enjoying themselves to the full.

In the middle of the night we heard a commotion and were told by our daughter's boyfriend that she had just gotten up and stormed out of the condo and out of the building. Fortunately we could trace her footsteps because it was snowing and bitterly cold. She had stormed out in just a nightshirt. We found her lying on a sofa on the upstairs landing of an identical condo building next door. None of us had a clue as to why she was there but her explanation was that "Mom told me to come and sit up here."

Our daughter was at the top of her class, a Berkeley graduate with a good job and no previous signs of mental illness. She had been outgoing and attractive to her peers. She didn't drink or do drugs so the break was an immense shock to all of us. We were so shocked in fact that we cut the vacation short and I returned with her to San Francisco where she lived, to get medical help. We had to drag her kicking and screaming because she saw no need to go home. She said she was fine. When we got back to the city she refused to go to the doctor and that's when I found out for the first time that because she was an adult, there was nothing we could do about it.

This began the worst days of my life. I couldn't stay up there. I was teaching and couldn't desert my students for what could have proved to be a very long time. She wouldn't speak to me anyway, so I returned to Southern California and waited for the call I was sure would come telling me that she was dead or involved in some sort of catastrophic accident.

Driving seemed to calm her and she would take off and blindly go wherever the road took her. Many times she called her brother, not knowing where she was or how to get back home. He would have to guess where she was from landmarks she could see and guide her home with the phone.

The call finally came in the middle of the night. A park ranger from Yosemite called to say that she was wandering in the dark and had lost her car. Fortunately for us, he was familiar with mental illness and set her up in a tent and gave her blankets until her sister drove the four-hour trip to pick her up and then the four-hour trip back to San Francisco in the middle of the night to bring her home. I thank God for her siblings, even though I consider myself a non-believer, because they were so good to her when she was in the throes of her illness.

The Yosemite incident finally convinced her to seek medical help. Despite many detours in her path caused by not having insurance, being out of work, and being extremely mentally fragile, she has taken her medication, completed her Master's degree and qualified to be a licensed therapist.

We are so proud of her. We know that her stability may only be transient but we are so grateful for it and we have learned how to live one day at a time. We love her so!

What is the best advice that anyone has given you?

Back off. Your child is an adult. Be there for her, but stop trying to take control of her life. All it does is create tensions between the two of you and intensifies her symptoms.

How do you continue to learn about mental illness?

I think the aspect of myself that I am repeatedly struck with, and struggle with, is the denial I continue to experience. You think you have it all covered and that everything is manageable and fine, and then there is another episode. The feelings that immediately emerge are the old 'out of control' feelings that stay with you, at least for me, until I can intellectually get a grip on myself, and start the process of telling myself to let go again. I have worked and worked on it, but have to continue to do so in the way I deal with my son when he goes 'off the wagon' and in the way I deal with the rest of my family and with friends, as well as the way I function as an advocate for him and others with mental illness, addictions, and co-occuring illnesses, and so forth. If I don't force myself to let go, which has gotten much easier through the years, I end up allowing myself to become completely preoccupied with the *not agains* and *what ifs* – all of the stuff you really can't do anything about. So, I continue to learn and continue to hope that I can get better at it and, in the meantime, I gain incredible strength from how others handle their situations. I am profoundly grateful for my NAMI friends who never judge and who are always supportive.

What impact did the use of medications have on their behavior, personality, body, relationships, outlook, life, and future? How were they changed?

At first, when our daughter was only suffering from OCD, the use of Prozac was very beneficial. It was almost as if she had never suffered from OCD as all of her symptoms subsided. When she started self-mutilation (cutting) and the depression and anxiety became an issue a few years later that became a real issue with the medication. She was not only on Prozac, but also a mood stabilizer as well as birth control for rather heavy menstrual cycles. Our daughter had almost a constant frustration with the 'lack of feeling' that came with taking the medications. As she came to the age where she felt the need to experience a sexual release, she found the medication had a bad effect on her as well. At one point she was hiding her meds for over a month. The outcome was that the depression and anxiety became much more unbearable. We felt as if we were in a no-win situation. On the one hand she did not like the fact that she didn't feel highs but felt very flat and on the other hand without the meds she was faced with her demons. We were actually starting to work on changing her meds when she took her life.

My son took Depakote while he was hospitalized for four weeks, and he gained ten pounds, which he disliked. He never talked about his meds, but of course we saw that it calmed him down, made him sleepy. It turned out that he never took any after that; he said the only thing he learned in the hospital was how to bring a pill up from his sternum!

Trying to learn about things, I went to a UCLA seminar for bipolar people (which my son refused to attend) and found a dozen very bright young men, and a few women, discussing their "cocktails." I was astonished at the quanitity and mad mixtures they were experimenting with to find the right combination for each of them, and to lessen their side-effects. I knew my son would have loved that meeting—you could feel the electricity of their manias in the air.

My son lived nine more years, accomplished a lot, and we were very proud, thinking he had beat his illness—or even been misdiagnosed in the first place! We never guessed that his demons were still at work, constantly telling him to end his life.

FAMILY, FRIENDS & MENTAL ILLNESS

When my brother and sister got sick it was like a nuclear explosion in the emotional terrain of our lives

What advice would you give to a family encountering mental illness for the first time?

I would encourage people to get as much information as possible--not just from the people working with your relative, but through books about the issues affecting him or her, and also through support groups. Support groups are probably the most important. My husband and I attended Al-Anon years ago and came away with a sense of relief that is almost indescribable. We were completely bowled over by the fact that no one judged us, blamed us, or told us what to do, and that everyone seemed to understand what we were experiencing.

Through the years, I learned some really profound lessons from relatively simple ideas. For example, when you find that you are working harder on your relative's problems than he or she is, it is time to step back and do something else, because it will never get you what you want. Through NAMI I learned that you can't know what no one has told you--which for me as a parent was particularly profound, because I always felt I should have all of the answers.

Speaking of NAMI, I became involved initially because, as a social worker, I felt it was a particularly wonderful organization for the people I was working with. Only later did I discover that I needed NAMI as much as my clients did, if not more, in some ways. I focused on my son and his alcoholism, but have always suspected that there is something else underneath the drinking. My father was a binge drinker with periods of untreated depression and anxiety as well. My maternal aunt had bipolar disorder and committed suicide. A maternal great aunt ended up in a state hospital where I remember visiting her with my mother, seeing my great aunt strapped to a post on her bed.

What were the reactions of your family and friends?

My mother and I had a relationship that was filled with anger; almost any contact between us for years had resulted in her fury and my fear of her anger. I didn't know until many years later that she, like my grandmother, suffered from severe depression. At that time, my father was my absolute hero, and again, it was many years later that I realized that the relationship my parents had was complicated by many circumstances, in particular, his affair with one of his students at the university where he taught. It almost ended their marriage.

My brother and I knew what was going on (my sister was only six at the time) but our mother's angry behavior had alienated us for a long time. The fact that no one, personally or in the world of psychiatry, had any understanding of depression left her essentially alone in her own home. My dad, on the other hand, was gifted and charismatic and we (and everyone, it seemed) adored him. In fact, my mother lived alone and isolated in her own home for many years. It wasn't until many years later, after she had died, when I began to understand about my own illness that I realized, with a sadness that will always be with me, that her life had been so terribly painful. I wish she were here now; I would be able to show her the love and sheer mercy that she was denied.

It really began in earnest when I eighteen and at Boston University. I had been doing well in school until my mother came up to Boston on business and wanted me to stay with her. At that time, parents, and especially the mothers of the child with the mental illness, were told they were at fault for what happened.

I have seen many things in myself and family members that alerts my introspection and causes me to wonder about how we see the current world of behavioral failure.

My mother has bipolar, my daugher-in-law has depression, my eleven-year-old grandson has Attention Deficit Hyperactivity Disorder (ADHD) and other disorders, I have had some sexual addictive behaviors, starting from early adolescence, my son-in-law has had some sort of mental illness that has caused some health issues, and I have seen others in my family tree who have some issues with brain disorders.

It seems the more I am aware of mental illness, the more I see events and circumstances that tell me we have only taken a short step on a long road toward full recognition of all of the behaviors that signal some form of brain abnormalities that influence our behavior. We must not think we have discovered all the forms of mental illness—much is waiting to be discovered about the things that hinder the human psyche.

As soon as we found out that our son was mentally ill, we told all of our friends and family. We provided an education about mental illness as we informed them. Every single one of them understood and was supportive. We were on a campaign to educate the world. What we found out was how many other people were dealing with similar problems in their immediate or extended families, but had never shared with us. We were surprised about how people kept this very significant part of their lives a secret. My son's siblings were better able to accept and deal with our son, knowing about his condition and mental illness in general.

What behaviors or symptoms caught your attention?

My brother is three years younger than I. As we were growing up, I didn't notice behavioral problems until he started middle school. This is when he started to get into trouble at school and with my parents. He seemed to say or do things that would attract negative attention. He would do the absolute opposite of what anyone told him. I wish I could say that I observed this behavior in an unbiased fashion, but my vision was clouded by frustration and jealousy. Why were my parents paying so much attention to him and none to me? I began critiquing myself and wondering what was wrong with me. For a while I didn't have any friends because I felt like, if my own parents didn't like me, how would my peers?

Has this condition brought you into new relationships or friendships, and if so, how and with whom?

Yes. Growing up, I had a relative. I did not live near him, so I did not know he had been hospitalized for depression at sixteen. I did not know he was not letting his parents see his home. I did not know he had no friends. Once his mom told me what was happening, I told her I was also passionate about art and gave her my phone and e-mail address, hoping he would contact me. He never did.

Then he came with his mom out to Los Angeles for my birthday and we had time to talk. I took him to see the Queen Mary. We have stayed in touch by phone and mail. He has a computer but does not use e-mail. I also invited him to join my husband and me to visit my brother back east. That is when we started getting closer and when I first learned about NAMI.

When I got home, I first went to a support group to learn how to help him and was referred to the Family to Family class. I finished that and read a couple of books on mental illness and sent them to his mom and dad to read. I have become close with them, and they are wonderful people. I have visited them in Kentucky a couple of times to help cheer up my cousin. I introduced them to support groups, but they have not participated.

My aunt did go to Family to Family and loved it. She is going to become a licensed Family to Family teacher. I can tell that she benefited from the classes in the way she handles my cousin, who has lived with her and my uncle for two years now. She lets his nasty comments and lies (exaggerations) roll off her back, and has stopped constantly asking him how he feels when she sees that he is obviously in pain.

Were you worried about how this was going to affect your family?

I was always worried about how my mother was affected by my sister's manic depression. During this time, she would always refuse to take medication. For over fifteen years my mother dealt with her daughter who suffered from this illness.

When my sister was depressed she would move in with my mother and when she became manic she'd become too much to deal with. Many times she would get arrested and put into mental facilities. She'd still refuse to take medication.

Thanks to NAMI, my family had the good fortune to attend their twelve-week Family to Family course. We also attended quite a few of the local support meetings that were held at Northridge Hospital. These people at the group meetings were people that had learned to work with their children, husbands or loved ones.

The people and the programs offered by NAMI provided my family with the necessary tools that were needed to help my sister. The Family to Family classes taught us what we needed to know and do when my sister was in trouble. It gave my family strength and support for one another. It really got my sister back. I can't say enough about the wonderful people that guided my family to where they are today.

How did or do you find mental or behavioral healthcare providers?

The police took her to a hospital where they put her on a 72-hour hold.

I had caught our son stealing his dad's Percocet (for a kidney infection—we never kept any drugs in the house, otherwise), and had called him a drug addict. I said I wanted to take him for some kind of rehab. He was infuriated. He said he wasn't an addict and go ahead, he'd go to the hospital just to prove it.

I called our therapist, whom the whole family had been seeing since our son's behavior got out of control, and he said take him to the hospital.

I told him I thought he was bluffing, but he wisely told me, "When a patient says, 'Take me to the hospital,' it doesn't matter why—just do it." I knew one of my girlfriends practiced art therapy, so I called her and she recommended Northridge Hospital, Adolescent unit. Off we went, and after a twenty minute interview, the doctor simply said, "bipolar disorder."

What have been your biggest relationship challenges with your family member who is mentally ill and how have you dealt with them?

My relative lies a lot. For instance, he told me that a woman on an airplane flight he took had a dog on a leash in the cabin. Another time he said his pet pug ate a lady's sandwich when he was visiting the retirement home where he takes his dog to cheer up the residents.

He lied about having a full-time job and that really hurt him because, when his part-time temp job ended, he was devastated. At first I just said "Really?" in response to his outrageous comments. Once he lied to me about having bathroom accidents (which his mom told me about because I was planning a trip to New York with my relative and she wanted to make sure he would not have an accident that would embarrass and upset him.) When I confronted J (which his therapist told me I should do), he denied it and then went upstairs and jumped all over his mom for telling me. I felt terrible about all that.

Then a fellow NAMI friend, a person with major depression like my cousin, suggested that I ask, "So how did that affect you?" when he makes an obviously untrue statement. He also suggested I make an equally outrageous comment about a similar thing happening to me. The first time I did it, my relative stuttered and said it really was not a big deal, and I think he knew that I had caught him. Then I felt bad for what I did.

I am still working on how to handle the lies. I think I will choose my battles and only address the lies that may hurt someone or cause my relative embarrassment.

I wonder what would have happened had my mother not been mentally ill all her life, and had been able to nurture me as a child, and how that would have changed the course of my life. Would I have been a better person or did the adversity that came my way provide the traits that I am so glad are part of me now?

I regret not knowing what it might have been like to have a normal mom, and a dad who was not so stressed that he could not attend to me as a father might have. He was always so angry. I regret that I was also angry and full of hostility and judgements as a result of the trauma of my childhood years. I did not recover from these things until I found NAMI. I found hope when I took the Family to Family class and eventually became an advocate, and now am more secure about what life means to me, and how I approach its challenges.

How did you recognize you were in a relationship with someone with a mental illness?

I was in my late thirties. It took about a year after my boyfriend's suicide to decipher everything. I'd known for some time that something was wrong. At one point I had told him I thought he might be mentally ill. He just stared at me. I knew something was wrong but I didn't know what. Three times a week I'd walk with a friend and I'd give her an update on his bizarre behavior. She couldn't make heads or tails of it either.

After counseling, going through all his belongings and paperwork, a pattern emerged. I couldn't deny the drug use when a year after his death, I received a letter from customs that they'd confiscated his medication and methadone. Talk about in your face. I'd been living with a full on drug addict and had no idea. I'm pretty sure he was also bipolar and the drugs made his brain really wacky. He was a total control freak and would do really weird stuff that didn't make any sense. One day he started driving to work and then came home saying his car was making a funny noise. It turned out it was a battery-operated mini fan in his glove compartment that had turned on. He said he stayed home from work because we were having problems. Huh? I told him he could use that as an excuse if he needed to, but why would he stay home with me if things were that bad? Sometimes he would open all of the windows in the entire house and it would feel like a wind tunnel. Once we were dining out and he kept taking my can of coke away and putting it out of reach (the only glass the restaurant had was a little tiny juice glass), so I had to ask him every time I wanted some. That was just weird. He said he was being polite. Huh?

He would come home from work yelling at me for some irrelevant thing. He would go out in the evenings for no reason and return hours later. He would make careless mistakes doing things around the house or with his motorcycles or car that he shouldn't have made. At one point he started taking a liquid supplement. The way he treated it and took it seemed ceremonial, ritualistic even. When a normal person takes vitamins, they just take them. He would take it out of the fridge, go into the garage, use the dropper to count out the drops into a glass and so forth. A normal person takes it out and squirts some in their mouth. There seemed to be no end to the bizarre behavior.

After he died, part of my healing process was that in my mind I went over every moment of the three years I was with him. He was going to bars. Oh, so that's why he was always late coming home from work- he wasn't supposed to be drinking. Oh, that's why he would come home and I would say, "OK, dinner in ten minutes," and he'd leave, saying he was going to Taco Bell, but really he was going for a drug fix and would come back two or three hours later. He had asked me to charge $500 on my credit card for car repairs. I wasn't comfortable with that. After all, what legitimate company would take charge card from someone who wasn't authorized? It turned out the auto repair shop was a front for the drug dealers. So he was telling me he was having a bunch of work done on his car, but it was obvious nothing was being done. He tried to tell me he was converting it to a race car. Yet the new engine he'd purchased was still sitting in the garage and all this money was going out. After he died I found bills for a bunch of stereo equipment he'd bought and probably used for drug payment.

What resources have you used to deal with mental illness and which do you value most?

My thing was trauma. I grew up with a schizophrenic parent and in my late thirties, my live-in boyfriend committed suicide. The whole thing didn't seem real and I kept expecting to wake up, because this wasn't on my list of things to do in this lifetime.

A strong support system of friends and family is the most important thing in healing. Thank God my baby sister came to my rescue and we became very close since then. She immediately flew in from two states away to stay with me. I was in so much shock, I couldn't even drive.

I took a multi-attack approach, that is, attack the problem from all sides in the hopes of equalizing it as quickly as possible. I found traditional counseling, group counseling and spiritual counseling to be very helpful. It took me three counselors to get one who really could help. The first two didn't seem to know where to start and didn't seem to understand what was reasonable and what wasn't. One told me to get a job at Starbucks so I would have medical benefits and could go to her indefinitely (hello! I have a master's degree). The next one told me to have the motorcycle sold by our next meeting a week later. Are you kidding me? This set me up for failure since I don't know the first thing about motorcycles, much less ride one. It took me three years to sell that damn motorcycle!

The thing that really got me through it was Survivors After Suicide (SAS) and their eight-week group counseling. Then I graduated to the once-a-month group. I went to that until I felt like I needed some distance from the whole thing. I still go a few times a year, like on the anniversary of his death and his birthday.

Is there anything you would like to share about your spouse's mental illness?

Twenty-five years ago I married a wonderful man. In my eyes, he was perfect. He was a recent college graduate full of drive and ambition, with a good heart and most importantly, in love with me. I felt I had chosen wisely and during the first eight years of our marriage we were blessed with two beautiful children. I thought life couldn't get any better.

Shortly before we were married, my then-husband-to-be told me about his abusive childhood in the hands of his stepfather. Although, it concerned me, I brushed the matter aside, thinking it had been worked out with therapists in the past. However, about fifteen years ago and after several failed business attempts, something was 'triggered' and I noticed a change in his behavior as he slowly fell into a deep depression. Depression was something I did not understand. I saw so many blessings in our life. Why couldn't he just snap out of it? On good days he was almost back to his old self. And on better days, he was pumped up and invincible. Little did I know that these drastic mood swings were not normal, but symptoms of a mood disorder. After years of seeing countless doctors and being on practically every drug out there, he has recently been properly diagnosed and appears to finally be on the right medications. My husband suffers from bipolar disorder but the road to finding the help he needed has been long and painful.

Bipolar disorder affects the whole family and in my husband's case the valleys and peaks were at times extreme. Having our children witness their father going from depressive to manic moods was very difficult for me. Watching him self-medicate with prescriptions accumulated over the years, suicide threats, his despair and hopelessness, sent divorce thoughts racing through my head. These were just a tip of the iceberg.

At the other extreme, the mania/hypomania would often come unexpectedly with reckless thoughts, actions, and words, transforming him into a different person which, for a time, was only compounded by his obsession with energy drinks. I feel that his impaired judgment and impulsiveness may have played a role in various failed joint-business ventures with undesirable individuals and in the decision-making process of other more conflicting and emotionally-charged matters. One was keeping our son in private school while we could have been saving and buying our home before we were financially ready. As a stay-at-home mom caring for our young children, he was the sole provider for ten years.

I often wonder if this added burden and stress during those difficult years were a bit much for him. His inability to hold down a job when he had one, failed business ventures, his undiagnosed condition all caused our relationship and finances to suffer. I recall my anger towards him. How could a man with so much potential drive me to such unbearable frustration? I remember thinking and even telling him how I wished he were a paraplegic instead of appearing to be a functioning individual because then I would no longer have to cling to hope.

Over the years, seeking and finding the proper medical treatment was not an easy task. Navigating through the County system during a time when we had no insurance was challenging, and finding a compassionate doctor who was not just a drug pusher when we did have insurance, was just as difficult. The key is to be properly diagnosed and receive the proper treatment. With mental illness, getting the right medication/dosage and or combination of drugs can be an arduous process. In my husband's case, it has taken years of trial and error. Also, as in my husband's situation, psychotherapy needed to be part of the treatment plan. I remember him taking the wrong meds for years and therapy sessions were inconsistent, if at all. Another key factor is the patient's acceptance that something is not right and willingness to want to get better. My husband has now taken on a more active role in his treatment and sees a psychiatrist who monitors his drug intake regularly and meets with a therapist once a week.

Looking back at all those tumultuous years, he did experience moments of lucid clarity. He found a spiritual connection with God and converted to Catholicism. Through all his trials, his faith never wavered. I found this deeply touching, inspiring, and humbling. He also went back to school and got his MBA. And although he has mostly held down blue collar jobs for the last four years, despite his work experience and education, he comes through every month in helping me pay the bills.

Working in the education/medical field for the last five years has helped me to better understand mental illness. I have learned to be more patient and empathetic and I know that he may require treatment for the rest of his life in order to keep things under control. When I look into his eyes, I see the man I fell in love with and married, and know he has remained a devoted husband and father. I admire his deep faith, his compassion and kindness towards others, his ability to forgive, his unconditional love, and how he works endless hours and multiple jobs just to keep food on our table. Over the years I have learned much from him. He is by far a better human being than I can ever aspire to be and I have decided that I am not giving up on this man. We recently celebrated and renewed our vows on our 25th wedding anniversary, surrounded by our children, family and friends, and although it did not come without some bumps along the road, I am more committed to him than I have ever been. I know that with the proper treatment, along with our love and support, he will one day live life to his full potential.

What impact did your family member's illness have on you and your family? How did you feel about the ways their illness impacted your life?

My sister got sick when she was seventeen and I was nine years old. It threw my family into a huge panic. My parents had nowhere to turn, and at that time the parents were often blamed for a child's mental illness. They went to specialists for her, and there was blame and turmoil in the house after that. I became the perfect child so I wouldn't get any of that negative attention, and so they wouldn't have any more to deal with on my account. I became an overachiever and felt very forgotten by my family for the most part. All of the attention went to her, and I was afraid of her because she was so unstable. I don't believe she would have hurt me, but I felt afraid if left alone with her.

I moved out as soon as possible, and never moved back home after college, even though I would have liked to. I didn't feel I could go home because my sister became very jealous of me and everything I did. I never felt like I had a home to go back to. On the plus side, I became very self-sufficient and still am very good at taking care of things when bad situations happen. I grew up and matured very quickly and am very capable of taking care of everyone. However trust is an issue for me, because everything in my house was so unstable.

My mother was always paranoid and thought people were out to get us. Secrecy was very important to her and it became the rule in our family. For a long time it made me very secretive about my sister being ill, and my mother filled my head with conspiracies. After she had her breakdown, I questioned everything she had ever told me in my life, including all of the lessons a mother teaches a daughter. I didn't know what was true and what came from her paranoid mind. I could never discuss anything with my mother because she would hang on to it for years. Later, I found I couldn't tell anything to my father, because he would share it with my mother. Therefore I had no one to share my questions and thoughts with. That was difficult. I felt like I had no family to lean on and that was a great loss for me. I grieved for the loss of my mother in my twenties instead of in my forties when she really died, because I didn't have her for all of those years.

My mother's illness impacted me heavily because I needed a mother so much and she wasn't there. Instead she was someone I had to hide everything from and someone I didn't want to talk to. Her illness caused her to say and do things that estranged us in my later years. The saddest thing for me was the fact that I was very close to her in my younger years and loved her deeply. I mourn her death still.

⚜

For me, having a brother and sister with a mental illness was devastating. Growing up, they were my heroes. They were my big brother and big sister, buffers between me and my parents, role models, and friends. When they got sick, it was like a nuclear explosion in the emotional terrain of our lives. We didn't know how to deal with it. And when we went to get help from the system, no one would lift a hand. We went to social workers, to the police, to the hospitals.

No one would do anything because, even though they had severe schizophrenia, they weren't violent. I could not understand how a system that I thought cared about human beings would turn it's back on my family. For me, it was a terrible act of betrayal. This was added to the sense of betrayal I felt towards my brother and sister. Of course, I knew intellectually they had a mental illness, that they weren't responsible for their behavior. But deep down I felt betrayed. I couldn't understand how the brother and sister I had loved so much, who had always stood by me and guided me and who I worshiped, now had descended into complete madness. They were now dangerous on an emotional level. They threatened me, they robbed me, their behavior was beyond my comprehension. Worst of all, I felt so helpless, because there was nothing I could do to help them. I felt like I betrayed them too, since I couldn't help. All I could do was put a lock on my door.

Somewhere along the line when I was a teenager, I promised myself one thing. I would never trust another human being as long as I lived. I would say it over and over again with such conviction. Some of that feeling was caused by my brother and sister, but most was caused by the extreme disappointment of seeing a system turn its back on us when my brother and sister suffered so much.

I felt great stigma too. I felt that I was disfigured in a way that couldn't be seen by just looking at me. There was such stress living in my house since I never knew what behavior would I witness. Would my sister start screaming at me in a psychotic rage? Would my brother be sitting in a chair, smoking a cigarette, oblivious to the world around him? Would my sister be in her room, blasting an Elton John album, playing it over and over again? The tension of those years was beyond anything I've experienced in my adult life.

When I got to college, I was always worried that I, too, might become ill, so I often saw school counselors. One psychologist I remembered seeing told me "If you don't come to terms with what happened with your brother and sister, I guarantee you this, you will never have a family of your own." His words were prophetic, since I've entered my 50s having never married. A couple of times I came close, but it seemed that deep down I always valued being alone more than being with someone else. That perhaps is the worst effect.

I also cut myself off from my past for many years. I would tell people that I was an only child. I simply didn't want to bring up my brother and sister, with whom I had lost contact in my early adult years. It was a tragic thing.

As an adult, I had to do some terrible things. When my sister began to abuse my elderly mother, I flew back into town. I set up a small apartment, but my sister refused to go. I had to tell her she had to leave my mother's house. I knew she would go no-where else but the street. I don't feel guilty about what I did. I thought I had no other options. A piece of you dies when you have to make such horrible choices.

On the positive side, I've never had the ability to ever consider that I was better than anyone. If someone had engaged in criminal or self-destructive behavior, it never bothered me. I could accept any past. As long as they weren't destructive with me and had stopped their criminal behavior, than I could accept them for who they were.

As bad as my past was, in recent years, I've been truly blessed. I decided to take a NAMI Family to Family class and it was here that I learned to my bones that my siblings behavior was not of their own design, but they truly had a biological illness. There was still a part of me that blamed them for their past behavior. But seeing pictures of how the brain was seemed to strike a resonant chord in me. It was then that I truly got it.

When I saw my brother and sister again, in my brother's case not having seen him for almost twenty five years, I was able to accept them for who they were and play a positive role in getting them services and showing them the love and support that I'm certain I would have been incapable of doing without taking the class. I was able to get them off the street. My brother even has a job now.

And that's why I'm writing this section of this book. I'm here to tell you that no matter how horrible things appear to be, miracles can happen, and your family relationships can be good again - provided you accept your relative for who they are rather than for who you want them to be.

YOU & MENTAL ILLNESS

I always accepted the fact that I had a mental illness..

How and when did you start to recognize that you had a mental illness? How old were you?

I knew instinctivly that I did not see things the way other kids my age did. It could be kindergarden age or my high school years. I never told anyone what anguish I was experiencing. Or how fearful and paranoid I was. I thought either they would not believe me, would lock me up and that would be the end of me, or worse, that everyone would know my secret. I always felt that there was something mentally 'off ' about me. From kindergarden age, I always talked to myself, had conversations with people who were not there, and I heard the voices. These voices sounded like Smurf sing-song-like voices. It also was like having a bad set of headphones on your ears playing a record backwards at blaring volumes that you could never remove. These voices could vary in tones, from harsh, dull tones, almost whispers, to horrific, booming volumes.

One thing is very present, even with me being in recovery mode today. The voices are in the background, always with me. But that is all they are, most days, just background noise, making it harder for me to concentrate on a task at hand.

As I approached the end of my seventeenth year, I found I could no longer contain the voices, depression, worthlessness, and hallucinations, to name a few things that I was experiencing. Growing up it was an inside family joke that when I got a migraine and was trying to reach out to my parents to let them know I was sinking, I would say, 'I need to see a headshrinker, you know, a pyschiatrist.' They thought it was for attention, and that nothing was wrong with their child. At least nothing serious, like a mental illness, like schizophrenia.

In hindsight, I did the best that I knew how under the circumstances. So did my folks. I'm an adult now. I have learned from my past experiences, good and bad. And I also have learned that I can only be responsible and have so much control over a situation/outcome. I can only control how I choose to act, or react. With the help of my meds and therapy (thank goodness!), I do not choose to live in the past. I choose to learn and glean some wisdom from the past. I want to make goals and plan for the future and live for today.

⚜

I knew that "something" was wrong with me at an early age, twelve or thirteen. My parents and I chalked it up to PMS .But that was not it.

⚜

I was thirty years old when I realized I had a treatable mental illness. Before that I struggled to maintain normalcy while still experiencing voices. I did not know what a great help medication could be. When the voices would get contradictory, I would think of myself as broken and get a good night sleep or call in sick to work. I had no idea I could live without the voices.

Was the realization that you were dealing with mental illness sudden and traumatic or a slow evolution??

The realization of mental illness came very slow for me. In the first thirty years of my life I really thought my dead relatives were talking to me. They guided me, they had secrets with me, and they lived within me. I comprehended ghosts and lived in a magical world. I functioned in society thinking everyone was like me. But when I went to my first psychiatrist, I learned the voices were an extension of my imagination.

It took a while for me to actually relearn how to think about the voices differently. I went to many therapy sessions and read the whole book of miracles. I realized I had made up all those voices. I learned to take it easier and not be hard on myself. I learned that it is OK to do nothing. Every day I accept my mental history in a new light. And take the next day as it comes. I try to hold on to these moments as they pass.

What's the biggest change mental illness brings to your life?

I was never so scared as when I was told by a therapist that I wasn't responding to the counseling I was receiving after my wife's suicide. To be told that I needed 'medical help,' not just someone to talk to, was frightening. I watched my wife battle with a barrage of medications and never really get better. The thought of facing that battle myself was almost more than I could bear.

Was there anything or anyone who presented an obstacle to your coming to grips with this condition? If so, what was the obstacle and how did you overcome it?

Yes, there was a person who presented a huge obstacle in my coming to terms with my schizophrenia....ME. And really getting to the point where I am now, which is recovery, I feel that there is most certainly stigma out there. However, the self-imposed stigma I did to my own psyche was so much more damaging to my self-worth.

It did not help my depression. I would put myself down, before others could do so at my expense. I would value other's opinions, even strangers', before I would trust my own. If someone said something, or looked at me sideways, it would tear me to pieces. I was Silly Putty in anyone's grasp. And it was my loss, because I knew I could be so much more. Not for others, but for my own self-esteem and my own sake.

I started putting a list on my bedroom mirror of happy faces, or making lists of things that I wanted for myself out of life. Such as respect, integrity, to trust myself and others, be more proactive, positive, seek out things instead of waiting around for them to come to me. I had also gained nearly 100 pounds due to, not only my meds, but lack of activity. I no longer felt like me, nor did I even look like me. I'll be honest, I have lost about half of the weight, fifty pounds. It has taken about two and a half years.

I will keep going. I still have days when I feel bad, or nothing feels right on, but I know that I am making progress. So, even on a really crappy day, if all I can do is roll out of bed and do a gentle walking DVD tape, I know I'm moving in a good direction. I say this because there is a mind-body connection. Eating healthy is great for me, but I found that I needed some daily structured activity to ramp it up.

I am very fortunate because I have a dad who, for the most part, tries to understand my position, even though he has a full life of his own. By checking in with him, and making an appointed time for us to talk about what's bothering me, or what is going on in my life, it puts me in a better frame of mind and gives me a fresh perspective on how to relate, where I might not have previously had that.

Do you find you structure your life around this condition? If you do, how do you do that and what impact has it had on you?

For me, personally, I have found that I needed to structure my life around how I am feeling that day. That can be emotionally, or mentally. There is a lot of gray matter in my brain - literally! Nothing ever appears black and white to me. I live with schizophrenia.

I was diagnosed half my life ago. I am now thirty-five years old, and I live with my dad. I'm fortunate to have him. Still, I have these grand visions of one day being totally independent. There is not a time when I am without the voices. However, that being said, they do soften their volume at times. And at this point I feel that I have schizophrenia, but it does not have me hostage some days.

I know that I have my personal limitations, whether it be the disease/disorder, or my personality traits that make it more challenging. I crave the structure because it gives me an outline of what to expect. For example, I'm a list-maker kind of person. So I have an organizer full of pages of lists of what needs to get done the next day, or week. I check those lists daily and mark off when a task or appointment has been done. I drive.

I'm fortunate to have a small group of friends that I have cultivated. Some know about my schizophrenia, and some I do not tell, for fear that they would not get it. Or would cut me off and no longer want me around their children. Maybe I'm the one who is not being reasonable and should give them the benefit of the doubt, but the stakes are too high, for me.

It was not until the past year or two that I slowly began to feel that being a person with schizophrenia is only one component of my make-up. It was then that I felt more comfortable in my own skin, and began to tell extended family members and some friends.

I have come from a place of not just realizing my limitations, but acknowledging my potential gifts. Having this hand dealt to me, I now feel it is not a death sentence. It is possible to date, and maybe one day, marry. Maybe I can one day hold a part-time job, and earn my own money. I have also become more insightful, observant, compassionate of others, and more aware of what's going on in the world as a result. However, like most of the population, I still can't balance a checkbook.

Do you feel that mental illness has resulted in dependency relationships?

I do feel as though some, or most, of my relationships are me depending on someone else. It can be a parent, a sibling, or trusting a total outsider's opinion over my own, when I am having a bad day. I live with the nightmare of schizophrenia. My fear is that my judgment is so uncertain about the most minute things, that on an off day, it's like, 'Who am I? My bones feel too big for my body.'

The voices are never nice. They are constantly putting me down, looking at the worst possible scenario. That kind of loathing and self-doubt is ingrained in me, and my relationships, and how I view my circumstances. But on a good day, I can differentiate that those voices are coming from me. They are from me, a part of me and my insecurities. Manifesting itself a thousand times over.

I have been trying to watch, not just what I say to the people around me, but also my tone. I'm working on cognitive behavior skills to replace the negativity with more positive thoughts. And when I think I am in the wrong, I have learned how to rectify it in such a way that is socially acceptable in the 'normal world' however one may define that.

Now in recovery, I concentrate on meds, therapy/physciatrist, and my environment and support systems. The more I am excited and motivated, the more things I find that I want to do, on my own. I strive for more independence, at thirty-five, and I think it's about not being afraid of succeeding, and about having the coping skills to know how to handle various situations that may come my way.

Sometimes it's too much. Sometimes I want it all. I have pretty realistic goals in mind, which require some help. And asking for that help is ok, because I know I'm moving in the general direction of where I really do strive to be. Why did I have to have schizophrenia? Why not me?

What was the first time you turned to medication to help you deal with your condition? What did you take, how much did you take, and how long did you take it?

I knew something was wrong, I just thought it was physical. I went to urgent care. After being examined, I was diagnosed with depression and given a prescription for Prozac. I also made the phone call to the county mental health department and set up a psychiatric appointment.

At first, the effects of the Prozac came slowly. By the end of the month I was having a party in my head. The psychiatrist asked me how the medicine helped me and I said "It makes the voices in my head happy. I'm just a little worried though, one of them is making jokes about killing myself." The psychiatrist told me right away that my condition was more serious than depression. He told me the voices were not normal and that he could help me live without them.

I had never known a life without voices. I was prescribed an anti-psychotic. I learned the voices were an extension of my imagination. Over the next few years I would take my medications off and on. When I took them I became happier and heard fewer voices, but I'd stop for a while until something happened, then I would take my meds again. Finally I was admitted to a mental hospital and was put on Haldol. That took care of the voices! After six months of Haldol and a great therapist I was able to switch and maintain a good attitude. Now if that extension of my imagination returns, I know it is time for me to cherish myself and heal.

It's really hard to find the right medicaton and to get the right dose. Prozac has been a miracle for me. I don't feel drugged and don't feel depressed. I've had to add Ritalin to help me concentrate and eating right and getting exercise really works.

How and when did you start to recognize that you had a mental illness? How old were you?

I was twenty five years old when I began to experience a strangeness of thoughts. I believed I was contacted by a higher power to take part in a great happening that I was central to. It took several years for me to recognize this was not real but rather a delusion which came on me lasting for weeks and months at a time. During this time, I was living alone in a remote coastal area in northern California. At first, these experiences of mood were a welcome addition to my thinking as they made me feel special and important. I imagined myself to be telepathic and a prophet of god. I believed I had extrasensory powers. While all this was somewhat fantastic to me, I resolved to study my experience like a psychology experiment. I began to see early on that I was unable to control my thoughts and so had no ability to have perspective. I <u>was</u> my thoughts. As time went on I recognized that I was unable to work because I was filled with thoughts about my delusion such that I could not focus my mind.

Was the realization that you were dealing with mental illness sudden and traumatic or a slow evolution?

Rather than accept that I had a mental illness, I got caught up in what seemed to be an 'alternative reality,' as I termed it at the time. The fact that I was mentally ill took years to accept. I normally had a manic episode once a year and it lasted for weeks. Each time after I 'came down' I would wonder if the experience had been real or not. They were, as if, religious experiences. That is, they had a spiritual or emotional feeling attached to them. Over the course of fourteen years, I began to see how these experiences affected my life in negative ways. I began to accept the idea that these experiences were not real.

Toward the beginning of my recovery, I began to see the illness in these experiences and after each episode I would hope they were a fluke and would not happen again. Finally after twelve years, I recognized the immutable fact I was mentally ill. Furthermore, I was able to resolve my confusion over whether these manic, religious-like experiences were mental illness or a rightous calling from God. I began to recognize that God didn't want me to suffer as I was and, though I wanted to be close to God, maybe God was saying to me, "No, Don, you can't sit next to me. You have to live life like any other person, with blind faith over a lifetime." That thought was able to heal me. If they weren't ordained by God, then the experiences were not valid. If they were not valid, then let go of them. They are part of the mental illness. This kind of thinking created my road to recovery which is now going on twenty five years.

If there were a long delay from the onset of the symptoms to the acknowledgement of the illness, what were the consequences of that delay?

The consequences of the delay in acknowledging my mental illness was the postponement of my recovery. As I began to gain more confidence that my condition was a mental disorder, I was then able to move forward with my life with less conflict or emotional angst. If I knew then what I know now, recovery could have come 10 years earlier. I probably could have had an effective healthy recovery much sooner. Instead, I stayed stuck in my delusional life, trying to resolve my dilemma of rejecting or accepting my symptoms. This is also true in my social life. It wasn't until I was well into recovery that I could date, finally meet someone to marry and have a family of my own. This is another factor that has helped me and could have sustained me in my recovery much sooner. With recovery came the ability along with the desire to be more social, to deal with the social anxiety which was well affixed to my fears of being rejected, as if someone would be able to pick up on my mental illness without me saying anything about it. This was the self-imposed stigma I carried with me and which was broadened by my delay in acknowledging my own mental illness.

Who or what are the people, resources, medicines, etc. that you find most helpful in dealing with this condition?

The people most important to me in my everyday life are my wife of twenty three years, my adult daughters and grandchildren, but also the professional colleagues I come in contact with. Being a psychotherapist, specializing in bipolar disorder, puts me in contact with others with this condition and offers me a chance to 'pay back' for what has helped me in making a life. My psychiatrist of many years is my mainstay in recovery by encouraging me to find my own solutions to life issues. As well, medication has made the difference in having a life and recovery for which I am grateful. In addition to all of this, the re-emergence of my creative side at the beginning of my recovery continues to this day. It lay dormant for many years and now is a source of great renewal for me. Music, writing, singing and mastering several musical instruments give me a sense of personal accomplishment. The fact that many mentally ill individuals have creative talent that goes untapped is a thing which spurs me on, to not waste my abilities. That I can bring this creativity out in others is important to me and increases my sense of satisfaction.

What made you finally seek help?

There is an inner force that seems to prod me on toward recovery. Usually it alerts me when I am nearing a moment of opportunity to discover something relevant to where I am in my life and the changes necessary in that moment that lead to a better place for me to be. I am then appreciative and thankful and uplifted in a way that cultivates the essence of my being, and drives me forward. I keep saying thank you, thank you, thank you.

⚜

From the time that I was very young, I always knew that I was 'different'. Not only was I adopted, but I just didn't think or act like other children or really anybody. From infancy I was a rocker. I rocked violently to soothe myself to sleep. This went on... well, I still do some form of it and I'm in my forties.

At age five, the obsessive compulsive behaviors started. I began to pray and count things over and over to ensure that I wouldn't die. By the age of ten, teachers were suggesting to my mother that I needed to seek psychological help. My parents tried but at that time there was no real help for someone so young, who was so severely mentally ill. By thirteen, I became very wild and did a lot of what my parents called "running the streets". I was overly sexually active, stole money, I was cutting my skin, and lied about everything. However, the real story is not what was going on outwardly, rather what was happening in my head. I was all tangled up inside. I was brilliant at school work. That came easy. Socially and emotionally I was dangerous. I played with drugs and alcohol but they made me lose control even further and I didn't like that. I manipulated both men and women with sex. For many years I lived my life as if I were trying to die. I was a risk-taker by nature of my mental illness. In high school, the anxiety set in and I suffered severe panic attacks. People laughed at me and thought I was on drugs. I got into physical fights.

By the time I was an adult, I was living a complete lie. I fabricated my whole existence. My mind was in a battle with itself and I was in pain. I was a guitar string wound up and ready to snap! I met a man and married him after knowing him for only three weeks. The marriage lasted a year. I left him by catching a ride on a semi-truck with a woman truck driver and ended up in Indiana. **That woman ended up beating me daily.** When I escaped from Indiana after a year, I returned to California, promptly dated several women and one man and got myself pregnant. I knew I was a mess. It wasn't until my son started showing signs of strange behavior at an early age that I realized I had to come to terms with my own mental illness in order to help him. When my son was eighteen months old, I was hospitalized and diagnosed as bipolar with OCD and anxiety. I was on the road to getting help. Although it wouldn't be for another five years until I started to see signs of real improvement in my condition. I did have the tools to succeed. I had a psychiatrist and the will to get better. At present, my son and I both live with bipolar disorder and manage to love and care for each other.

⚜

What have you learned about this illness?

I wish I'd even known that Obsessive Complusive Paranoid Disorder (OCPD) existed! Somehow, somewhere, I stumbled onto it on the web, and a big light bulb went off. I think mental illness is not discussed openly and often enough, anyway; but it seems like schizophrenia and bipolar disorder are the 'sexy' mental illnesses that everyone hears about. While OCPD, NPD, BPD and some of the other disorders almost go under the radar. There's a perception—I've even read it in articles by mental health professionals—that these illnesses aren't as disabling. Perhaps a 'light case' of OCPD is not as disabling as a 'light case' of schizophrenia. I can't address whether that may be true. But if you love or live with someone who has OCPD, especially a severe case, you know that it negatively permeates every aspect of one's life, and often makes it impossible for the OCPDer to hold down a job. If you add the hoarding aspect that some with OCPD have as well, it can be physically dangerous to everyone in the home. Yet you cannot have someone committed to a mental health facility for hoarding.

What is the best advice that anyone has given you?

I asked a person I have known all my life. I wondered about saying "no" to all of the ugly things in life; mental illness, poverty, injustice, neglect, addictions of all types, saying "no" to all of the negative junk that comes at us every day. The response was, "Well, for you and me, we can only say, Yes." That was so profound that I had to ponder it for a long while before I understood, and now it has become part of me.

What symptoms caught your attention?

When I was growing up I often felt a disconnect from everyone around me. However I was usually just considered super-sensitive or moody. It wasn't until I was an adult, and the depression really surfaced, that I could look back and identify my childhood behavior as a manifestation of the depression.

In my late twenties I had a few episodes of feeling completely numb, and often unable to get out of bed to function normally. However, I still was not diagnosed as suffering from depression because, well, it just wasn't identified in those days. It wasn't until my first child was fifteen months old that I could identify a very significant feeling of numbness, of loss of interest in almost everything that used to fulfill me - my work, my husband, my music - even my beautiful little girl. It was only then that I was diagnosed with Clinical Depression and my treatment of medication and therapy began.

What are your proudest moments dealing with mental illness?

Teaching a seminar on mental health issues to rabbinic students in the seminary and opening up about my depression. Allowing those students to begin to open up about their personal experiences with mental health issues and to not feel stigmatized by it.

Also, by talking openly while my children were growing up, they were able to talk about their mental health issues in an open manner at a very early age.

How have you managed to become a successful advocate for yourself or for the person with the condition?

Talk openly and honestly about depression, no differently than I would if I had asthma. Stay on top of all the newest findings and read as much as possible about the disease.

How do you see yourself today, and how has that image been changed by this condition?

Frankly, as much as I sometimes despise having to live with clinical depression, I think it has made me a more caring and thinking person. I tend to look into other people's "eyes" more, to see what might be going on within a person beyond the surface.

I see myself as someone who can help others face the truths in their lives and help them see how they can live fulfilling lives in spite of the mental health issues that may wear them down.

I was kind of surprized when I found out that it was not 'normal' to think the people on radio and TV were talking to me and sending me secret messages. I thought I was special. When I found out that it was just a symptom of my mental illness, I was disappointed. I missed that feeling of being special. Well, I am special, just in a different way.

How has the reality of the illness affected the way you engage and interact with others?

By the time I was fourteen, I was already having difficulty interacting with others. I was having manic episodes but did not realize it until much later in life. I had a hard time adjusting to the peer pressure of friends, fashion and cliques at school. It was junior high when I didn't seem to fit in. I got in fights. Most of the time I provoked them and felt as if I were a loner. My parents didn't have the money to buy the expensive fashions that I felt would have helped me fit in at school, and so I was made fun of.

Along with feeling alone at school, I felt alone at home. My imbalanced family life left me more depressed than ever. My parents were always fighting and I was the punching bag. I was hit and beat by my father for unknown reasons. My mom was an alcoholic and I was embarrassed by both of them. I didn't dare bring anyone over to the house, even those who were close to me. Not only was I an only child, but I was living on a farm nearly thirty miles outside of town, and miles from a close neighbor. Socialization did not become my strong point as I developed into a teenager. The gawkiness, awkwardness and my illness all played a part in what I became.

After several manic episodes and an attempted suicide, my father took me to several psychiatrists and psychologists. I don't remember the visits, nor do I remember what was being offered. I know I was prescribed Desyrel and Prozac, and after a brief time, I seemed to do a bit better. Soon after this I began my cycle with drugs and alcohol because it made me feel cool. No one bothered me at school and my peers seemed to leave me alone. I felt as if I could do anything and I felt like I was so popular.

I continued through school, barely making it sober, if at all. I skipped some school and partied with anyone and did whatever drug was available. Although I was on the track team in high school and becoming increasingly popular with people, I still felt awkward inside. I wasn't comfortable with myself or with the majority of people. I would occasionally overreact to things and blow up on people, places and things. These manic episodes seemed to come and go, and I always thought the reason I would have them was because of someone else's doing. It was their fault because of something they did, said or acted. It was never my fault. I tried to be someone I wasn't while drinking, and I was scared people would find out. They could see right thru me, but I thought I was the great pretender.

I graduated from high school, my parents divorced, and I drank more. I went to a junior college and took some classes but was not retaining any knowledge. On my eighteenth birthday, I threw a huge birthday party for myself. The cops were called. I jumped out of the window and was arrested in a bush for being under the influence of a narcotic. After doing community service, paying my fine, attending meetings and staying sober from drugs (but not alcohol), charges were dropped.

I then decided it was time to skip town and start a new life elsewhere, but my dad decided that it was time for me to live with my very church-going Aunt in Sylmar, CA. I knew I needed to get away from the drugs and begin to grow up, so in 1990, I moved in with my aunt and uncle. Unfortunately my behavior did not meet with their strict rules. After one night of drinking too much, my aunt decided that she had had enough of my behavior and kicked me out.

I was enrolled in college but don't remember a lot of it. I worked and don't remember a lot of that either. I made friends, but unfortunately they were more like people you hang out with at a party, not what I would call real friends. I had stopped doing cocaine and meth when I moved to Sylmar, but continued with pot and alcohol. My episodes became more frequent and I lost friends because I would 'freak out.' None of them seemed to understand what I was saying, so I avoided telling my true feelings until days when I would blow up. It was embarrassing and regretful, and I felt like I could tell no one about my feelings for fear of shame. None of the party people I hung out with would understand, nor did they care. So I hid my illness and grew independent, as I felt like I could trust no one. I didn't want to be judged, ridiculed or made fun of, so I didn't tell people.

By the time I was twenty-three, I married a man I met in a bar. He didn't have a job and was here in the United States illegally. This caused more friction in our marriage as he was unable to get a decent job without a green card. I worked a regular job and some part-time jobs to make ends meet for us, but it was exhausting.

I stayed with him for three years, but my episodes got more and more crazy, and I found myself blaming my depression for a lot of things. I would think, "If only he would understand what I was going through." The fights and bickering got to be too much and, after an exhausting suicide attempt, I moved out.

I was on a downward spiral. I was under heavy pressure to keep myself together. I felt like there was no way out and I had no escape. I never let myself drink in the daytime because I had to keep my job, but as soon as work was done, I drank and drank. In a world of over six billion people, I felt alone and like I had no family or friends. At this time in my life, I was still reeling over my parents' divorce and was particularly angry at them. I know they had their own issues to deal with, and I didn't let them know what I was going through. I felt like the only way out was death.

I had tried suicide a couple of times since I was fourteen, and really never could bring myself to do it. But on this particular day, I was done with living. I was on top of the 210 freeway where it connects to the 405, and I was going to jump. I stopped and got out of the car.. the wind was rushing up on my face, drying my tears as soon as they were coming out. Something inside of me said, "Your life is worth it," and I felt peace. I got back into my car and admitted myself into a psychiatric hospital.

Finally, I was doing well and the medicine finally seemed to work. My spirits were being lifted. I still felt alone, like I couldn't talk to anyone about what I felt inside for fear of people thinking I was a freak. So I never talked about it. I finally went to a psychiatrist who suggested that I had a drinking problem—finally I heard something, and I began my sober journey. It was four months after I left the hospital that I got sober and have remained sober ever since.

When I was thirty, I met my new husband and we had a whirlwind affair, and soon after, I was pregnant with our daughter. When I first met my husband, I tried all of the same old stuff with him, but it just didn't work. After long and tiring episodes that seemed not to change my husband, that's when I began to change. I began talking about how I felt and what seemed to drive me nuts, and he would give me inspiration and tools for what to do with people, places and things.

Soon, I developed friends who understood me and what I was going through because I could talk openly and not be embarrassed about it. But it was my husband who understood me and I felt I could trust. I told him everything. He knew what medications I was on and could tell when an episode was coming up, he would divert me from it. It was uncanny how he could see me going through one and I didn't even think I was! It was my husband who changed me, although I was changing in small ways. It was him whom I trusted, and then trusted others and could engage with others without freaking out.

I can hold down a job and have terrific friends whom I can talk to. My illness changed the way I interacted with others because I was ashamed of my illness, ashamed of being scrutinized, made fun of or judged. By growing older and learning from my past and having a loving relationship with my husband, I could love others. I didn't really have a reality until I got sober and really learned about me. So, having any type of relationship with anyone was close to impossible. It wasn't until I learned to listen and control my tongue, that I could have a meaningful relationship with others. Until I understood that my disease wasn't really me, then could I learn and explore its effects on me and others. That's when I could know when I was freaking out, or when my disease was taking over. But I truly feel that without my husband helping me, I would not be in the place I am today.

What impact has mental illness had on you and your family members? How has the illness affected your relationship?

My relationships have obviously been strained by my mental illness. From my teens into my young adulthood, I had a tendency to overreact to almost everything, and straining any relationship because of 'their' problems. I blamed everyone else's behavior for why I was so explosive. If people would just do things 'my way' everything would be just fine and the world would be a better place. My inability to live in reality strained all relationships, because the reality was, no one had to do things my way.

I would put myself into unhealthy relationships because those were all I knew. And if the relationship was somewhat healthy or normal, then I would taint it with all of my nonsense. Needless to say, all friendly relationships became a battleground for my behavior. My parents put up with me, because I was their child and they had to. I am not fully aware of what they thought about my behavior at that time, but looking back on it, I knew it was a mess. I think if I had not been their child, they would have chosen to stay away from me. My aunts and uncles kept their distance because I was a tormented teenager who had too much anger bottled up inside and ready to explode at any time. I had fits of yelling at people for what I believed they had done wrong and for their bad decisions. I drank too much and became a lush and no one wanted me around. I partied hard and I paid the price, as the only friends I had were my party friends. And if they acted out I would sever all ties with them as well.

I was into my late twenties when I did I finally clean up my act and get sober and make amends to my aunts, uncles and anyone else I could remember attacking. But the relationships had ceased to exist. I developed a better, closer and hopeful relationship with my parents and they with me. When I was in my 30's and had my daughter, I developed an unconditional love for her. This was something I had never experienced. I embraced the love I had for my husband after four years of marriage and our life and relationship took a turn for the best. I love him as deeply as love can be. He understands me more than anyone else and knows and understands my moods, my emotions and my ups and downs. I find that I can tell my husband everything and he will navigate a way to tell me if I am wrong or right in what I am expressing. He is a great listener and a great helper for me to understand my own thinking.

Sometimes I don't understand why I am thinking some irrational thought, but he can investigate where it is coming from and put me at ease. He has been a great influence over my healthy relationships and has encouraged me along the way. I owe a great deal to my husband for putting up with someone with a mental illness. Not all people would take this on and marry someone who has issues, but he has and has done it with love.

What do you tell yourself about yourself, and how do you keep that 'self-talk' healthy?

I remind myself that depression is a disease no different than diabetes or asthma. It is not about my emotional maturity, it is about a disorder in my brain. When the depression hits and I feel out of control I try to remind myself that "it is the depression talking". If I can't remind myself of that my husband will do so.

The other thing I do is read, read, read about the depression. Understanding it as a disease and reading the words of others really has helped me learn to live with it. It is especially helpful to read about famous people who live with it so that I am reminded that it can happen to anyone!

When are the times that you feel most hopeless?

Major stress is what brings on my depression and when I feel that I have no control over my life I feel hopeless.

I hate being ruled by my depression. Life is hard enough and sometimes when I'm depressed, people think it helps to tell me to "cheer up." It doesn't help. I don't like being told how to feel. Sometimes I just need to go through all the sadness and the hopelessness and cry and get it out. Then, I can feel better. I know there is hope.

What's the biggest challenge mental illness brings to your life?

I have a cyclical depression disorder as well as social anxiety. I take medication which is controlled by a doctor. I find that taking the right medication has helped me cope in all that I can do as well as therapy. I discuss my fears and talk about ways to combat them. Depression and anxiety bring me additional challenges in making it in this world.

I am sympathetic to others with the same plight and want to show people how to cope with their disorder. The challenge that depression and anxiety bring me is having to deal with things without isolating and without worrying about it.

How have your coping strategies changed over time?

Coping used to be copping out, not dealing with feeling and using drugs. I don't do this anymore. I have learned to feel the pain and move on from it. This is a daily process and changes over time. You combat one problem and another comes up. I stay away from the drugs and alcohol and anything that can make me feel not in control. I let myself feel the pain. I do not dwell on it and do whatever I can to work with it so that my challenges become positive, not negative and detrimental to me.

I take classes in spirituality and push myself to attend group-type things. Social anxiety has caused me to isolate myself. I am aware of my discomfort but push myself to attend things where I know I will be safe and hope to join in those activities where I may not be "so safe". It is ever changing and it's all good. I like that and that I work on my challenges.

What is the most important skill you have learned in dealing with mental illness?

I remind myself that depression is a disease and not a reflection of my personal worth or abilities. I read constantly to remind myself that it is a disease that impacts a great many people, young and old, rich and poor, male and female.

I also keep in mind that educating myself about the disease and talking to others helps me feel like I have some control over the depression rather than always feeling that it controls me.

DRUGS, ALCOHOL
& MENTAL ILLNESS

When I was high or drunk, nothing else mattered.
Not the pain, the hurt or anything, and I could escape.

What was the first time that you either took a drug recreationally or began to take a controlled or prescription drug without, or in excess of a physician's order?

I was in my early twenties when my boyfriend (an attorney) gave me some cocaine to try. It became a habit on the weekends when we went out. At first I loved it. We played board games with friend and we had fun, I was not my usual shy self but outgoing and confident. But then I started having anxiety attacks and nosebleeds and I got scared. I missed work every now and again. That didn't affect me too badly.

My first two years using cocaine where not bad - I enjoyed the rush but hated the anxiety. It went away after I finally went to sleep. I realized it then that I had a major anxiety disorder and this brought it out. I stopped doing cocaine for nearly eight years until another boyfriend introduced me once again to the stuff. So began the fifteen year habit of ups and downs. I used my prescription drugs to keep me 'down' when the anxiety hit. I was able to function for a long time as others I knew both at work and at play were doing the same thing.

I was in eighth grade when I started using cannabis. I was doing it recreationally with other school friends. I never thought of any serious consequences that could come from it. Any time I did it, I was in the company of friends making not so good choices.

What did you take, how much did you take, and how long did you take it?

I took everything and anything. Pot, acid, pills, but my favorite, the one I enjoyed the most was PCP. I started smoking it at the age of thirteen and at the age of forty was still smoking it. I'm now forty-eight and have not smoked it or done any other drugs (except for my prescribed meds) for six years now.

Did you start taking this substance on your own, did someone turn you onto it, or did a physician initially prescribe it?

I started in the sixth grade, with a friend. Her grandmother used to give us pot. The pot was her dad's, but he was seldom around, and grandma would just put some in a lunch bag and tell us to go have a good time.

Why did you do drugs? What did you think you were going to get out of it, or did you even think about what you were doing?

I took drugs because I liked them.

It was the cool thing to do. It made me, me. I really never thought about it. That was one of my biggest problems. I would always act first and never ever think about the consequences. Even when I knew what the consequences would be, I still did whatever I wanted. I didn't care. Actually, I did care, but for whatever reason (perhaps being bipolar) couldn't stop myself.

I did it so I could escape my reality. I was beginning to remember pieces of my childhood. I was beginning to relive some of it and I didn't want too. I didn't know what was happening to me. So, a friend of mine was a drug addict and I asked her for a hit of crack cocaine. She said I'd feel euphoric. I felt nothing. I had to try it five times before I felt anything and when I did, I was hooked. It did what I wanted it to do. I didn't think about anything but how great I was feeling and then after that went away all I could think about was the next hit.

I liked getting high and the taste of cocaine in the back of my throat. I felt invincible but did not really think of long-term consequences. There were times I got very anxious and could not sleep. I stopped using and then went back to it after three years or so and kept a fifteen-year habit going strong. I was able to live my life, i.e. work for a long time until it started to affect my lifestyle. I would not give up my behavior and tried to fit my other lifestyle into it. But, I was missing more and more work and couldn't hide the fact that I was doing drugs.

How did you get what you took? What did you have to go through or do to get it? How did you pay for it?

In the beginning, it (drugs) just always was around with friends, parties, friends of friends. As I got older and my drug use became addiction, I did pretty much everything. I would steal something from a store, and then return it without a receipt, and get cash back. I started dealing drugs, then started dating drug dealers. Then, I started to walk the Blvd. I started turning tricks on Sepulveda Blvd. The funny thing about that was I never went out there when I was high. I found that just walking and getting picked up, wondering whether or not I would get busted, was a high all by itself. Living on the edge.

Was this a conscious attempt at self-medication? What were the consequences of that decision?

A conscious attempt? Yes. You see, back then, there wasn't a lot out there about mental illness. When I was in the eighth grade, my mother placed me in the only psychiatric hospital I think existed at the time. There were the adult and young adult ward, the adolescent unit, and the ICU. I was there for three and a half months, diagnosed with 'unsocialized regressive reaction of adolescents.' What is that??

No, I don't believe it was a conscious attempt. I just wanted my pain to go away and that seemed to do it, for a short time.

I did not make a conscious attempt to medicate, although I wanted the pain to go away. I didn't know what the pain was, nor did I understand my actions at the time. All I knew was that I was hurting and wanted it to go away any way it could.

 My first result was to smoke pot and drink, because this made me so out of it, and I could laugh at all of the stupid things happening around me. I actually thought I wrote better term papers while high, but then I would re-read them later and couldn't understand what I was saying. This self-medicating behavior lasted until I was twenty-six years old, when I finally got sober. Until then, it was a downward spiral of doing drugs, getting drunk, using people and not caring about anything except my next high.

The consequences for self-medicating were a lost childhood and early adolescent years. I grew up too fast, learned things I shouldn't have known, and did things I shouldn't have done. As a result, I was labeled a troublemaker by all. I was only coping the best I could with the tools I had, but these tools were broken. I did not have family that intervened.

They turned a blind eye to the entire scenario. I kept a lot of my abuse hidden and thus, my parents did not know the pain, the drug use, or the illegal behavior. It got me into more hurt because I had no one to talk to about anything; I had no one to trust, no one to give me hope, and I ended up alone, confused and abused.

Did you find yourself spending a lot of effort, thought, time, etc. on getting or affording more of the substance you were abusing? What did that do to you?

Yes, I sold all of my belongings. I put myself in danger trying to get more money for drugs. All I wanted was the pain to end. All I wanted was to be free from my mental illness. It made me crazier. I hated myself even more.

What impact did your drug use have on your behavior, personality, body, relationships, outlook, life, and future?

It made me very "manic-y" as a young teen and I ended up having an episode which led to my mental illness diagnosis. It changed me because it came to a head with my lack of attention in school and it made me see I was on the wrong path. Had I not had the episode I would have had a graver diagnosis.

Luckily after I lost contact with these friends and went to doctor and took prescription medication along with my family's support, my counselors noticed a new person and I got better grades in school.

What did you lose and what did you gain from your drug use?

I lost sleep, a lot of it. I lost time because I just wanted to stay home and do the coke. I went out to get my drugs and I went out to join friends (not really friends, although I did not admit this to myself). I had terrible anxiety attacks and I lost jobs and my self-esteem became less and less.

I had a fifteen-year habit and I gained experience and the knowledge that I did not want to anesthetize myself any longer, but this happened after a catastrophic event. My boyfriend committed suicide. He lived in another state and when he came to visit me at Christmas I had a foreboding of disaster. By this time I had stopped doing drugs for about four months and he just couldn't get onboard with the new plan.

He bought me a ring for Christmas, which I returned to him and asked him to leave. After a major scene and my changing my phone number, I found that a week later when he had returned home, he shot himself in the head.

After you stopped using the first time, did you start up on something else? What was it and how long did it take to go from one to the other?

My drug of choice was PCP, used on a daily basis for years. Then one day my best friend/customer asked me for a 'front'. I told him he could have some free of charge. But, he was from the old school, so he said he didn't have any money - but he had a quarter gram of 'speed'. I told him to keep it, but he insisted that I take it. I did, put it in my jewelry box, and forgot about it.

Two weeks later after staying up all night, and having to go to work (yes, I had a very good job at a corporate office), I decided to try the speed out. Wow. It took me out of my PCP haze and I got so much done at work, at home, cleaned my car and still had energy. That quarter gram lasted me two weeks.

Less than six months later, I was up to using at least a gram a day and had gone from snorting it to injecting it. What normally took me one hour to do at work, now took me two hours, because I would tweak, organize, and re-organize, and re-organize everything again—all unimportant stuff. My paper clips had to be sorted, my pencils sharpened just right. It got so bad that unless I had my morning fix, I wouldn't go to work. I would hunt down my connection, and usually stay on Sepulveda Blvd in some cheap motel. I got so far behind at work and the reason was obvious to all that worked there. They decided to implement a new procedure, random drug testing.

What happened when you tried to stop using what you were taking? How long did you use before you tried to stop? What made you try to stop or to finally seek help?

I used cocaine for about fifteen years on a daily basis and finally stopped when I no longer wanted to live the lifestyle I was living. I moved away from those I felt were toxic and drug absorbed and stopped taking drugs cold turkey.

It was nearly a year that I had been drug-free when I slipped for about a week. That was back in 2005 and I have have not touched cocaine since then. I no longer wished to have the anxious feeling nor to spend my money or waste my time. I wanted to do things and knew I had to give this up. I did without repercussion and was lucky in that I was able to do this with only a few scrapes and scars. But then my fiance, whom I had broken up with due to lifestyle changes, committed suicide and I had and still have that road to travel. I live with this but after five years am now happily married and life a clean and good life.

While this was not my fault, it was a major wakeup call in that he was bipolar and was not taking meds and the drugs he used crossed his wires and caused this terrible, awful thing.

5

ENCOUNTERING THE LEGAL SYSTEM

You don't 'have an encounter' with the legal system.
The criminal justice takes over and has a life of its own.

Was there any build-up to your encounter with the legal system, or did the situation come out of nowhere?

When my son turned twenty-one, he was in college and evidently had a huge drinking party to celebrate that he was now of drinking age! The night ended up in some sort of episode that involved him jumping on a parked car and falling down. He was subsequently sued by the owner of the car for damages to the car, all of which both he and his girlfriend denied. They steadfastly maintained that nothing had happened to the car, but the matter went to court and he was charged with damages and received some sort of fine, I believe. We got help from an attorney friend so that he had legal representation, and we paid for someone local as well.

Nevertheless, he was found guilty and had to pay a fine, as well as damages, to the owner of the car. The whole situation was very strange because we never felt like we knew what had actually happened, and we were still inclined (yeah, denial is hard to give up) to believe our son and question the credibility of the victim. There have been two other legal involvements: the first DUI almost ten years ago, which involved a night in jail and six months of various groups and classes, plus, of course, suspension of his license for a year. He got his second DUI a little over a year ago, and spent seven weekends in jail, paid a fine, and his license was again suspended for twelve months. He recently got his license back and can drive his car, but had to have a breathalizer installed in the car for another twelve months. Hurrah! His father and I are appreciative of the laws in the state in which he resides.

We have learned a little something through the years and now will not help him pay any of whatever monetary repercussions he suffers from his drinking. But it took us a long time, even though intellectually we knew that he needed to be totally responsible for whatever happened as a result of his binge drinking.

Why, when and where have you had to deal with the legal or criminal justice system as a result of a loved one's mental illness?

My son stopped his meds, smoked pot and ran away from his board and care. He went to Santa Barbara and was arrested three times in one week. Once for vagrancy and resisting arrest, and once for getting in a fight outside of a bar, and then finally for using a credit card he found in a lost wallet. He thought he was justified in using it because he had lost his own wallet earlier in the week. He continues to think that the man who lost it was responsible for his troubles, because if he had not lost it, my son would never have been able to use the card!

He was arrested and charged with a felony. I found out where he was because I filed a missing persons report in Santa Barbara because he used to go to school there. Even though I am my son's conservator, I was not allowed to be there when they plea bargained with him. They convicted him and wanted to release him with time served and probation for three years. I begged the judge not to release him onto the street and instead let him be transported to a mental hospital. He refused. After a few days out, my son was arrested for looking suspicious walking around Montecito with only one sock and no shoes on his feet.

He resisted arrest, was tasered several times and placed back in jail. This time he was charged with not reporting to his probation officer or to the mental health center as he had been instructed to do. He appeared in court weekly and I went weekly begging the judge to let me transport him directly to Cedars in Los Angeles. Each week the judge would give me some excuse. Finally one week we went to court and the regular judge and district attorney were off that day. The district attorney said, "I think he needs to be in the hospital" and that was that.

After lots of paperwork, I paid for his transportation and he was in Cedars for seven months waiting to get into an IMD (Institue for Mental Disease). He's on three years probation, but all reporting can be handled from here by whatever treatment program he's going to. If he is not arrested for three years, we can probably get his conviction expunged. If he is arrested, the nightmare will start all over again. While he was being held, they had two psychiatrists evaluate him, and they both felt he was competent to stand trial. I since learned that competent only means that you know who the judge is and can sit quietly through the proceedings.

If they do send you to the state mental facility, they have a mock courtroom set up there to teach the defendants about how to sit in court and then they send them back for trial. In jail they offered my son meds but since he refused them, they did not make him take them. He had to be kept in isolation much of the time because he was annoying the other inmates. By the time he was released, he had a bushy long beard and very long wild hair, and he sat in court playing an imaginary guitar throughout the proceedings.

We used the public defender and he made himself very accessable to me. I also communicated closely with a laison attorney from the Los Angeles County Court system, since my son is conserved there, who was assigned to try to help me and my son. This entire experience is the most emotionally wrenching experience I've ever been through.

Why, when and where have you had to deal with the legal or criminal justice system as a result of your mental illness?

I am currently thirty five years old, sober since July 18, 2010. I am on probation for trespassing at a strip club in May of 2009. I'm due in court in Van Nuys, CA [Los Angeles County] on Sept. 3 to show my proof of twenty six NA meetings. At that time, I will have my probation completed and then request that it be expunged from my record.

I feel that the media needs more attention devoted to the good things that people with bipolar have done and can do. So, although I am contributing my horror stories here of being admitted to the psychiatric hospital four times and to jail once, I want this to be balanced with what I have done well with my life, as a bipolar person.

- I earned my B.A. in Global Studies, UC Santa Barbara in 2002.
- I earned my Notary & Real Estate Salesperson's License 2004.

- I completed courses to take the Real Estate Broker's License 2004.
- I was pursuing a Masters in Education with a Teaching Credential in Disabilities
- I worked as a Short & Long-Term Substitute Teacher & Summer School Teacher
- I was one of most popular girls in school, especially 8th -12th grade.
- I was voted "Most Eligible Bachelorette" at my ten year High School Reunion
- I worked as a Legal Secretary for many Prestigious Law Firms
- I worked as Concierge for two Private Airports for Celebrities & Fortune 100 Companies

My First Time In Jail & 4th/Last Psychiatric Hospitalization - Age 35 (4 Days):

During a mania in May 2009, I was arrested and processed through the jail system from 7 pm to 3 am. My family and ex-boyfriend scrambled to bail me out, but instead, within two tofour hours in a jail cell, where I was isolated for unknown reasons, I was evaluated by two men from the Mental Health system. It was determined that I was unable to care for myself, so they dropped me off at a Psychiatric Hospital in Orange County. Why so far away, I don't know. They forced me to receive a tranquilizer shot and numerous heavy-duty tranquilizer pills and released me after four days.

This was the 1st time I had ever been arrested and the 1st time I had been hospitalized in a psychiatric hospital in 13 years. So, you can imagine how much this decreased my confidence that I had acquired on how to control my mania, at least to the degree that I would never be hospitalized again.

What I didn't realize was the importance of SOBRIETY to maintain my sanity. I knew that I should not be drinking alcohol weekly and smoking weed almost daily, but I had a prescription for the weed and was living with my boyfriend of four years who smoked it daily for a company that promoted it in their business, so I rationalized my use.

My First Psychiatric Hospitalization - Age 22 – (3 Days): I was hospitalized for the first time for mania at the Psychiatric Health Facility in Santa Barbara, CA when I was twenty two. My eldest sister and current brother-in-law dropped me off. The staff decided that I was not able to care for myself. I was held for three days on a 5150 hold, and then released with prescriptions for Depakote and contact information for a psychiatrist and psychologist. I didn't know what was wrong with me and I had never heard of bipolar. I called a man who was at the last "party" I attended and he told me the weed we all smoked was laced with ice (the purest form of meth), I was shocked, but relieved, that I had discovered the reason for my mania. My very stressful and lonely life also contributed to it. I decided not to take the prescribed meds or see the doctors.

My Second Psychiatric Hospitalization - Age 22- (4 Days): I was hospitalized again a month later for four days at the same place in Santa Barbara. This time it was by the police. I don't recall the details, but I think I was running around my ex-boyfriend's apartment complex topless during the wee morning hours. I don't know why that made sense to me at the time. I think it had something to do with promoting equal rights for women to be topless along with men, but maybe it also was due to a combination of what was going on in my life and what was not going on in my life. I was given meds, stabilized, and sent home with the same prescriptions and contact information to see a psychiatrist and psychologist. I decided that I was still reeling from the laced meth and didn't end up following any of the hospital's instructions.

My Third Psychiatric Hospitalization - Age 22 – (2.5 Weeks): I was hospitalized a month later for 2.5 weeks, again at the same place. This was also by the police after my father flew over from Hawaii and my eldest sister and current brother-in-law answered my late night phone call. I called from a beach pay-phone asking for their help, since I had become homeless and didn't have anywhere to sleep. They had been waiting for my call and immediately drove to Santa Barbara from Ventura, called the police and the mental health evaluators, who determined that I was unable to care for myself.

It is VERY claustrophobic to be locked up in a mental hospital and jail. TORTURE! When I got out the 3rd time in three months, I was determined to do whatever it took to stay out of the hospital. So, I took the meds, saw the doctors and got sober. I had never considered myself to be a heavy user. The difference between a few drinks of booze and NONE was LIFE OR DEATH for me.

This lasted for about two years. I then stopped attending AA and taking meds, but I was very careful about my lifestyle, trying to be stable, not party, etc. That went on for about six years. Then, I almost died from a Vicodin OD when I was drunk and furious with an ex-boyfriend about who he was flirting with at the bar. He was too drunk to realize what was going on, so I fell asleep with a handful of Vicodin in my system, after telling him that I was killing myself. Thank GOD I woke up the next morning. I felt like I was dying, told my boyfriend to take me to ER, and after hours of suffering, I survived. That's when I realized I needed to start taking meds again (Lithium) and moved in with my mom, second step dad, and younger sister, who was attending college for her BA in Human Development. I needed to stay as far away from my ex as possible. He brought out the worst in me. As a Bipolar, we are EXTREMELY SENSITIVE to our environment and everything overall. I find that I can be so 'fearless' when it comes to calling out 'elephants in a room', but can't handle uncomfortable temperatures, uncomfortable clothing, annoying people, redundancy, repetition like taking a shower daily, etc. It's like a dog's hearing. They're overly sensitive but they can bark their head off and annoy everyone - except themselves. It's a mixed experience.

I wish everyone in my family would be sober and attend AA or NA and possibly take Lithium too. Some are sober but don't take meds and some are sober but don't attend meetings and some used to be sober, but now feel like they want to control it. The bottom line is that addiction and mental illness has caused a lot of pain in my family and I want it to stop. I have expressed my concern to them. In the meantime, I am trying to lead by example.

Believe it or not, (call it "grandiosity" if you want), but I have aspired to be the President of the United States in 2020, ever since I was twenty one years old. I realized it is not a realistic goal, since I am bipolar, don't have a law degree from an Ivy League University, etc., so that's why it's a DREAM.

In retrospect is there anything you could have done to have avoided or minimized your encounter with the legal system?

In retrospect, there are many things I could have done to have avoided or minimized my encounter with the legal system.

To sum it up, I would say BE EDUCATED, mostly by NECESSITY of being 100% SOBER, with the help of the NA, AA and the 12-Step programs.

It would really have helped to have an improved K-12 public school education program. I believe that basic living skills (including learing about our legal system) should be taught, starting in the most formative years. I learned everything the hard way, by experience. I didn't realize I could go to jail for a citizen's arrest for trespassing. When I was trespassing at the business next door and told the police I would be HAPPY to leave. Nor, did I realize I would get charged with multiple felony possession of narcotics because I left my prescription bottle at home and put all my pills in one convenient unmarked bottle.

Regarding my NEW life, I'm 100% SOBER! I finally took a "Newcomer's Chip - less than 30 days", which is actually not a chip, it's a white keychain that says "NA" on one side and "One Day At A Time" on the other side. I took it on my 11th meeting because I didn't want to bring that kind of attention to myself. I didn't want to go up and hug someone weird, etc.

I don't have a home group yet. I have seen many of the same faces at the different group locations, but I definitely don't feel at home anywhere as of yet.

I'm also having trouble getting a sponsor. I don't want to rush it and then have a bad experience, but I'm so lonely without my ex-boyfriend, no female friends, no family in this city, etc. A few guys have hit on me but I either don't like them or I feel like they will bring me back into drama. I don't want to drink booze again, have anxiety or have sex too soon with all those dangers.

I was heavily involved in AA after my third psych hospitalization. I didn't really consider myself to be an addict. I didn't want to be hospitalized again, and I knew AA might help me make friends who were sober, healthy, etc., since all of my partying friends disowned me. I was living in a "dual-diagnosed" cheap housing apartment that required meeting cards. At the time, I felt that I was living there because it was the cheapest place I could find so I lied and said I was an alcoholic just to get housing.

I had a sponsor, was sober for several months, went to lots of meetings, etc., learned a lot, but never really believed I was an addict. Besides, I was only twenty two. I felt way too young to stop partying. Now, at thirty-five, it's easier, but not that easy, for sure.

I feel like I'm in a really deep part of the ocean. I'm wearing scuba gear and am required to come to the surface slowly, so I don't die from that thing they get if they come up too fast (with the hyperbaric chamber or whatever). I feel like I have to relax, because there's nothing I can do to make the process go any faster. So, although I'm very uncomfortable, I'm trying to appreciate where I am and have faith that my life will get better (as long as I stay sober, in addition to my meds, exercise, getting a job, getting female friends, etc.) The problem is that there's more to my nightmare scuba analogy. I know once I FINALLY reach the surface of the water, I will be in the CENTER of the Pacific Ocean, all alone, and I will have to swim back to the Santa Monica Pier and get a bus back to my apartment in Burbank, so I have a lonnnnnnnnnnnnnnnnnnnnnnnng way to go. That's how I feel. Like I'm deep, deep, deep down in the center of the Pacific Ocean, all alone, with scuba gear, and it'll be a year or so before I get back to my apartment.

The GOOD NEWS is that hopefully, with tears welling up in my eyes, HOPEFULLY, I WILL BE HAPPIER THAN I AM TODAY. If this is what it's like for ME to get sober, it's gotta be a LIVING HELL for someone to get sober from meth and heroin or situations like my uncle and dad had with Vodka and homelessness. But, I am bipolar in ADDITION to being an addict to booze/weed, so this "dual-diagnosis" makes it very lonely, sad, and difficult for me. It seems my uncle and dad had/have bipolar also. They have shown all the symptoms including the extreme highs and lows from at least age eighteen onward. They both were very generous with whatever they had. Both were very spontaneous, spiritual, silly, but they could also be very brutally honest with their criticism and very verbally/physically abusive to their spouses/offspring.

It was very difficult to understand them. I can relate. Sadly. Slowly, very slowly, over the decades, my family has learned of the many, many people who have lived and the many who have died due to alcoholism and/or bipolar disorder and/or a combination of the two: "dual-diagnosis." The rest have struggled with panic attacks, anxiety, depression, and/or DUI's, Rehabs, abortions, theft, etc., but managed to move on with their lives without hitting 'rock bottom.'

I am currently realizing the life-or-death importance of being a SOBER BIPOLAR. This includes: attending NA 12-Step meetings and participating fully, taking meds two times daily, seeing a psychiatrist at least bi-monthly and a psychologist at least bi-weekly, getting exercise and sunlight daily, eating healthy and sleeping eight to twelve hours daily.

Helping homeless people can be rewarding. Say hello. Be of service. Call (877-Ask-LAPD) to get them emergency shelter, give them a dollar if you have it, and NA/AA Schedules and phone numbers. Tell them to call 211 from a pay phone for more referrals, etc.

It's hard to know what came first; the bipolar nightmares or the addict nightmares......Now I realize they came at the same time, around age thirteen, but I wasn't diagnosed until twenty-two for bipolar and thirty-five for addiction....... I didn't BELIEVE my dual-diagnosis until I was thirty-five....Believe It Or Not, I Still Don't Want To Believe It.......I Want To Believe That My Problems Are Based On The Fact That God Hates Me. If GOD would LOVE me more, I would be BLESSED with lots of money, a perfect spouse, several biological children, a huge home, a newer car, a better body/ face, a career to love, pets, vacations, etc.

I'm far from perfect, but I'm not lazy or evil. I have always WORKED HARD, so why am I suffering so much?? WHO KNOWS. All I know is that I LOVE YOU, I appreciate you, and all my loved ones.

What impact did your encounter with the legal system have on you and those close to you?

The question as written above is inaccurate. You don't have an encounter with the legal system. The criminal justice takes over and has a life of its own.

I don't think anyone can quite imagine the stress of trying to save someone you love from a prison sentence. When someone with a serious mental illness is making choices that keep bringing themselves to the attention of law enforcement, exercising extremely impaired judgment, committing offenses that are being taken seriously with grave consequences that are frightening and horrific, it becomes a matter of life and death.

It's your son and you will fight for him. You are his Dad. It is years of struggle, work, money, daily crisis, strategizing, finding solutions, winning, losing, being treated fairly, being treated unfairly, 'whatever it takes' to try to help this young man you love who has a serious mental illness - from going to prison. Prison feels like the abyss. The battle is all-consuming and takes precedence over one's life, business, and the time left for the other people in your life that you love - your wife, your other son, your daughter, your friends. Eventually your friends can't take listening to it all anymore and they're gone. That comes with the territory. And you haven't found NAMI yet.

You are reading this and saying "this guy's co-dependent as hell." And maybe you are right to a degree… It can get that way, but mostly it's just too damn hard to let go of that memory of a healthy young kid you once knew with all of life's possibilities in front of him. And then you learn that all those expectations just don't matter anymore. You learn that just moving forward, some growth, some peace, a better day, is what's important. You just want him to be safe, get the support he needs, recover, get well. And you know that if he would just agree to treatment he would have a shot at being OK. You know this, in the pit of your stomach, because one day you get a diagnosis and he is given some medicine in the hospital. You watch as the boy you love transforms from a broken human being almost unable to speak, nearly catatonic sitting on a chair in a locked, acute inpatient ward, and in a few days he starts to get better. Soon he is talking again and can shoot some hoops with you at the hospital basketball court and beat you at HORSE, over and over again. He's a good shot. You know something else too. You know that if he could adhere to a treatment program, take the medicine he needs, get the therapy he needs, have someone really help him with his issues, he could have a life.

You know your son. You know his heart. Who he really is inside. You watch when he is in treatment and you see with your own eyes that the choices, the things he did that got him into trouble would never have happened if he had been in treatment. So that's the answer. I'll fight for treatment. And then you realize that the criminal justice system is just starting to figure this out. One would think that with all that has been written about 'best practices,' they would actually be widely practiced. You learn that the law is part of the problem too. It isn't just resources. You learn that you can be part of the solution in his case, and in the system. You have become an advocate.

6

ENCOUNTERING MENTAL HEALTH & RELATED SYSTEMS

The Mental Health System is nothing like the general health system. You must educate yourself about the resources that are available.

What are your impressions of the mental or behavioral health system? What's good, what's bad, what needs to change?

Public and government support seems to be dwindling every year. The system was stretched twenty years ago when I became disabled. I became disenchanted in the public system. Now I use my Medicare to pay half of my psychiatry and I pay the rest out of my pocket. Any public assistance is rare. The good news is that there have been great research findings recently that can help people with their treatment. And of course there is support through NAMI to help find resources.

How have you found support for yourself? How do you take care of yourself as you deal with these responsibilities?

My daughter and I could not have accomplished what we have without government services and NAMI. AB3632 and SSI/SSDI have given her services and support she needed. And NAMI has provided me with services. I know I am not alone. I have resources. I have support. In order to give back, I now teach Family to Family class. I no longer take things my daughter says or does as personally as I did. I also realize more than ever that her illness is not my fault. I enjoy my life and enjoy being with her so much more now. Thank you, NAMI!

Have you ever run out of a medication you could not immediately replace? How did you deal with that?

My son was released from the hospital early, against doctor's advice, because he was granted a hearing and persuaded the judge he was capable of caring for himself outside the hospital.

The doctor refused to provide him with a prescription on his release. He said, "If he's going to talk his way out of the hospital, I have no more responsibility for him. Let him go."

I tried to go to the local pharmacy to refill an old prescription, but we had changed insurance and it would cost over $800 for thirty pills.

I went to the Psychiatric Emergency room they would not refill the prescription unless they could see my son. Of course, he refused to go and insisted he didn't need the prescription anyway.

Again, I called the hospital he had been released from and explained we needed a supply of his medication. But since he had been released, they could no longer provide medication or services for him and they could no longer talk to me. I begged to speak to the doctor but he was not on site and had left for the day. Then I turned to our son's former private doctor. He was kind enough to gather up some samples of medication and give them to us. It got us through the next few days.

Now that he has gone through more crises than I'd like to count he has medical coverage through his disability benefits and a reliable supply of medication. He won't take it. I keep it on hand though, just in case.

When systems fail, what happens?

Although we sought treatment for our daughter through regular therapy and psychotherapy and medications, there is an aspect that I feel could have helped us see the signs that she may have been contemplating ending her life. This was her school. After the death of our daughter, and only then, did we learn that there were pieces of a puzzle that if the teachers had pulled their resources together may have warned us of the potential for suicidal ideation. See, our daughter when asked if she would ever consider suicide would say no. No, she wouldn't do that to her horse. Or, no she wouldn't do that to her boyfriend. Always the answer was 'no'.

What I found out after the fact is that she had written a paper on depression for a health class the week before where she addressed the fact that she suffered from depression and was presently in a worse state. This is not something we knew about or would have even guessed. In English class she had to interpret a poem. She chose one about a woman talking of her soon-to-be death. The Dean of students asked her to look at the writings on a back hallway wall where it sounded like someone was contemplating suicide. (This was actually not our daughters writing but was inappropriate for the Dean to ask her to look at it and try to help). Another past teacher, who actually DID send me an e-mail, was concerned that our daughter seemed down and wanted me to share with her that he was there for her if she needed to talk.

If the school had a plan of action they may have helped us save her life. If one teacher was alerted by her homework and was able to put a red flag up that other teachers would be able to take note of, then the other teachers may have also paid more attention and said, "Hey, I'm concerned about this child too." A call could have been made to us. Even though our daughter was not showing signs of being in a particularly bad state at the time, she did have one bad day. That one bad day, she went in her room around dinner time and ended her life. If I had received a call from the school saying we have concerns, and knowing she was having a bad day, I may have watched her much more closely. I may have prevented her from taking her life. I believe all schools should have some kind of 'flagging' system when they notice that a child's work is turning dark, or openly expressing a deeper level of depression.

What should other parents know about your interactions with health care professionals and other mental health resources?

Parents... the mental health system is nothing like the general health system! You must educate yourself! In many cases there are facilities that are run by professionals but the counselors they use are students who must earn their hours to get their degree in counseling. Some are very good and some are novices. You as a parent must have your eyes and ears open. Don't just send your child in to talk with someone without interviewing them first. They may not be the right fit for your family. You may have to wait (unless you are in crisis) then insist on seeing whoever is in charge. Ask for what you want. Get ALL of the facts. Take the time to speak to the counselor alone and weigh your options for your child. This is especially important when choosing a psychiatrist who may or may not be prescribing medications. Go on the internet and research those meds. Your local library has free internet access. You must be diligent in becoming an expert in your child's illness.

Don't be proud! Take advantage of the resources. They are not for you. They are for your child. Apply for all that you can and wait as long as it takes to receive them. This is a life-long journey and things will add up. Your child may seem fine now, but there may come a time when he/she needs in-patient services and if you have set up the proper state medical insurance, you may not lose your house. **This can happen when all of those medical bills start rolling in**.   Keep in mind... when filling out these forms, they are for your child! You are looking to their future when they become an adult and may need supplemental security or some other form of aid. Start the ball rolling now when they are young. It is a long process.

Remember that health care professionals are people too. Mostly, they deal with adults who can be unruly. Be kind to them and let them know that you want to help them help you. Let them know that you are going to monitor everything about your child and hope to have great communication with them.

Lastly, and perhaps most importantly, record everything! Keep a log and keep every stitch of paperwork from school, doctor, legal, hospital... everything pertaining to your child. That is proof you are doing it all above board and RIGHT! Good Luck and God Bless!

RECOVERY

I believe most fervently that recovery is possible.

I have seen it happen in my own life. Taking small steps towards goals you desire can change your life significantly for the better. I have gone from a point where I was acutely psychotic to having a life that is satisfying. I believe it is possible for others to do the same.

In your opinion, is recovery possible?
Why do you believe that?

In my opinion, there are several ingredients that make recovery possible. Most of all, persistence and tenacity. Never take 'No' for an answer. Secondly, take your meds and stay on them. A social support system is important. Don't give up. Hope is as important to recovery as the air we breath. Lastly, recovery is defined by the individual. What may be important to you may not be to someone else. If you want it, recovery is out there for you. And though it may sound self-serving since I'm a therapist, getting into therapy with a good psychotherapist can help aid your recovery and offer you someone who can guide you in your recovery.

I believe recovery is completely possible. As someone with the illness, and as someone who functions at a high level of academic and artistic thought, I completely support this claim. I have had the illness for seven or eight years now, and by the time of my last episode I completely suppressed it myself. My hero is John Nash, the protagonist of *A Beautiful Mind*. It is difficult to explain how I did it, but I will try ---

I've had two episodes which went out of control, however every time I had an episode I learned something new. The first time, I learned to restrict my action and not verbally react or physically act on my delusions. This did not solve the problem. My first episode resulted only in a partial recovery which due to some inappropriate health care led to another flare up the following year.

Although I had learned to restrict my actions, my delusions came back. I count this whole traumatic year-and-a-half as one prolonged episode. After this I received better healthcare and made a full recovery, I went for four years without an episode and earned a bachelor's and then master's degree. Yet, in the back of my mind, lying dormant were my delusions. After I graduated with my masters, physical and emotional stress from my environment combined with some minor drug usage, caused my delusions to return. This was bad, when I got out of the mental hospital I was in, I recollected all of the thoughts that I had, sorted through them and began to refute the delusions.

This last out-of-control episode taught me how to restrict my own thoughts. Delusions are a hard thing to simply refute, but when a patient can recollect how their mind functions when it is healthy, they can restrict their own thoughts too. The last time I felt my delusions returning I did two things which are now my rules for preventing my illness from taking control of my life. First, I called my doctor, and then, I meditated on restricting my thoughts. I forced myself to think about things like compassion and well-being, and I preoccupied myself with art, music and my other hobbies.

As soon as I saw my doctor, I received an adjustment in my medication, which helped the sorting process and meditative dispelling of delusion.

Is recovery possible? Ah, good question. I think some people might think that recovery means that someone is on their way to wellness, or already there. It implies that there is no longer an underlying condition. I don't think so. I was diagnosed with schizophrenia and will probably always be a person with schizophrenia. For me, recovery means that I can get better, but not cured. How much better I don't know.

In the beginning I felt trapped in my own nightmare. I had no hope. Much to my surprise, now I am often described as high-functioning. I work hard for my wellness because I want to be the best possible "me" that I can be, and because it gives me hope.

What are the most important element(s) to recovery?

For me, the way to go is some type of structure that I can see myself doing, without a lot of pressure or stress.

1. Meds
2. Stablepositive/uplifing environment
3. Therapy/psychiatry

How have you managed to bring yourself up from the bottom?

The day I decided to stop doing drugs I began to shape my life in a better way. I moved away from the worst influences and did not frequent those places that I knew would tempt me into further distress. I had yet to hit bottom, although this was a really low point in just making the decision not to do any drugs. I hit bottom when I intended to commit suicide and then I knew I was in real trouble.

I was in so much pain and had really nowhere to turn. Someone made an offhand comment about getting into therapy and that's when I began looking to a suicide survivors group. Then after the eight weeks of the group I continued to attend the monthly program and began to see a therapist two times a month. My therapist gave me the tools to start helping myself. I look for avenues to use my time where I could start to experience some joy. While I was far from joy, I began to do at least one thing for myself every day. I started getting involved in spiritual and meditation groups and classes. It got me out of the house even if I had to really push myself to do so.

From there I began to get involved in activities that involved my interests. This included saying affirmations every day, many times a day, and keeping a journal when possible. I also wanted to give back to those who helped me and trained to be a Suicide Hotline Counselor. I worked the hotline for a little over a year. This was tremendously rewarding.

After about three years I felt that I was able to find a healthy partner and after only a couple of toads I found my prince. But that still does not cure me of whatever ails me. That keeps coming up from the bottom - knowing where I have been and never wanting to go there. I still heal from the many wounds, but am no longer on the bottom. I am far from it.

I learned to play solitaitre. It's something I can concetrate on – it helps get the focus off me. I don't have to be positive, I don't have to think, I just have to find the right card.

How do you deal with mental illness?

In dealing with mental illness there are three factors that have been continuously vital to the level of recovery I have experienced. The first is medication, although not 100% effective in all cases, I believe that the continued use of advanced psychotropic drugs has limited the number of unhealthy thoughts and delusions I experienced.

Medication became part of my personal hygiene and religion. In addition, the fact that I never ever miss a tablet reassures those around me that I am responsible and want to be healthy. Even when I feel I need an adjustment in levels of medication, I know that I am doing the right thing.

The second factor that has led to my recovery is good health care and psycho-therapy. My doctor is like my mentor, and I completely trust him. He allows me to suggest ideas for medicine, and has a brilliant Socratic method that he employs to allow me to awaken myself to what I need to do to ensure that I stay healthy.

The third factor is family and friends and the community. My family has its problems, as most do, but when it comes down to it, and even when they mess up a little they want me to be safe and healthy. Staying grateful to the community around me is a double-edged sword. I feel that having positive people around me is nearly as important as psychotherapy and medication usage. It is also my responsibility to avoid negative people. Some people will never respect people with mental illness, no matter how well they are most of the time.

What resources can you share to help others deal with mental illness?

THE ROAD TO RECOVERY GUIDELINES FOR MANAGING A MENTAL ILLNESS.

In 1979, I was diagnosed with bipolar disorder. I had a good job, a good family life, and what I thought was a good doctor, who prescribed an antidepressant. He gave my wife and me what we thought was a good plan for my wife to intercede, if she thought the illness was getting out of control. Two years later I shot up into a medication-induced mania (the plan failed) and my poor judgment and erratic behavior caused me to lose my job.

I got a new doctor, began taking Lithium along with an antidepressant, and my moodswings calmed down. However, the shame and consternation arising from my manic behavior and the loss of my job had thrown me into a tailspin. I made no efforts to prepare for the rest of my life. I was either making futile efforts to regain my job, or wallowing in a depression that the medications couldn't handle. My wife thought that this was the way I was going to be for the rest of my life (and I guess that I did also) and in 1983 we agreed to divorce. This happened mainly because we had insufficient knowledge of the true consequences of the illness and how to handle them, and no one to turn to for help (even today most psychiatrists don't fully appreciate this aspect of recovery).

The situation is better now (1997). However, someone who is as inexperienced as I was almost surely doesn't know what steps to take to properly manage their illness. Therefore, I offer these guidelines:

1. **Find a psychiatrist who specializes in your illness.** Proper medication management is paramount. It may take a while to find the right doctor and the right medications for you. Persistence pays off.
2. **Interact with others who have your illness.** Only then will you be with people traveling the same road as you, many of whom will be further along that road and can give you good, practical advice. This can be done in self-help support groups like DMDA (Depressive and Manic-Depressive Assoc.)

for patients, NAMI (National Alliance for the Mentally Ill) for families, and significant others in more formal groups led by a mental health professional. (Beware of ineffective groups that exist just to satisfy a clinic's protocol.) If one group doesn't suit your needs, after several meetings, search for others. Again, persistence pays off.

3. **Search for additional mental health care.** A doctor who sees you once a month to monitor your medication is not enough, especially at first. You need a psychologist or therapist well-versed in your illness to educate you, give you feedback on your symptoms, help you to deal with adjunct issues, help you manage your illness and provide psychotherapy when appropriate.

4. **Educate yourself.** The more you know about your illness, the better you will be able to manage it. Read books and attend lectures. Keep a mood chart and/or diary. Take an active role in your treatment.

5. **Establish your close support group,** and include them in the previous steps. Mental illness is not something that can be managed well alone. You need understanding people who can help you get to the doctor's office when you don't think that you need to go (a common stage of the illness), or are too depressed to care about receiving treatment. Overcome your resistance to accepting help (another common stage).

6. **Reduce the stress in your life.** For those of us with a mood disorder, this is especially important.

7. **If your illness has taken away your primary goals in life (as happened to me), find others.** I have found that having proper life goals has been vitally important in the management of my illness.

8. **Medication and therapy can only do so much.** A balanced diet, exercise and an active and healthy lifestyle are also important. Think positively. Act like you aren't ill, and one day you will be acting no more.

9. Trust. Don't stop taking your medications because of the bad side effects; it may take your doctor a while to get you stabilized on the right drugs. Tell your doctor everything that is going on in your life. Believe the knowledgeable people around you when they tell you that your symptoms are better or worse.

10. **Have faith.** You will have to accept whatever recovery your illness and treatment will allow for the time being. New medications, treatments and coping strategies are being developed every day.

Proper management of your illness is the goal. Your illness can be successfully managed, even if in your present state of mind you cannot possibly imagine how. You will make little progress until you finally decide to get serious about managing your illness. It took time, effort and the help of good people for me to get a handle on my disorder. Things got worse before they got better, and they don't always go smoothly now. I accept this and move on to do the best that I can.

2010 Update: All of the above still applies except that the DMDA has changed its name to DBSA (Depression & Bipolar Support Alliance). The rest is still as true and reliable as when I first wrote it in 1997. The Road was at a lower level and rougher than I would have wished between then and last year, but then came what I call, 'The Great Awakening of 2009.' My life has changed dramatically! There was no new medication, no new doctor, no new organization, no new tactic. Around the middle of the year, however, there was a new me starting to take shape and the change is still happening. All I can say is that faith and persistence have finally paid off. Now my major goal is to work to see that this change is not reversed. I will redouble my vigilance at working the tools above.

This does not feel like the 'up' side of that rollercoaster ride we have all taken. If it is, however, and the "down" side comes next, I will just redouble my efforts again, that's all. Good luck to all of us.

Who or what do you find most helpful in dealing with this condition?

I found that diet and exercise along with my medications helped keep me from hearing voices. I would cook a whole grain hot cereal for breakfast every day when I felt broken. I called my multi grain breakfast "Happy Food" because if I had eaten it that day, I had a better chance of being happy. When I was younger I used to walk a lot and that helped. In my thirties I started Tai Chi exercises. I began slowly working on improving my posture. The slowness of Tai Chi also brings a feeling of grace.

Now when I feel achy or mentally challenged, I will straighten up my back and lift my head slightly. This small movement can relieve tension and pain. I usually avoid sugar, but my brother-in-law recommended a cure for depression - "go for a walk in the sunshine and buy a chocolate bar."

The best resources I have are the medications that helped me to get out of my safe world after tragedy struck and the support groups and therapy I have been in. They help to reinforce that I can keep going.

Being with people that are like you and support you are a key to survival. To keep yourself away from those toxic persons who want to keep you down is the choice you have to make. I decided that I did not want to feel bad anymore and would do everything I had to do to change that. Survivors After Suicide was very helpful to me personally and my therapist and my husband are the greatest resources I have. It is my self, my determination, and each forward moment that keep me going.

I resent that I can't be normal without my medication. I resent the fact that I have to take it every day, but I'm better when I do.

Were the effects of medication as expected? Did you want to continue those effects even after the reason for the medication or prescription had been resolved?

One of my loved ones was on Zyprexa. It was shocking to see how much he ate. It was like he was a Tasmanian Devil at a buffet. He just couldn't stop eating, and his weight grew and grew.

They changed him to Abilify and he lost 100 pounds over the course of a year and half. In addition, he became much more animated. Before he never initiated conversations and rarely spoke. While he still is very quiet, he sometimes asks "How's it going?" For me to hear that, it's like a miracle.

What was the promise and what were the realities of medication? How long did it take to see the difference and what caused you to see it?

I think families have too great of expectations regarding the effects of medication. While medication sometimes addresses all of the symptoms, sometimes it doesn't address any. With so many, it seems somewhere in between. In my family, it has taken away almost all of the 'positive' symptoms of hallucinations and disorganized speech. I still occasionally hear some delusions, but they are more rare over the past couple of years. It's the 'negative' symptoms that seem to last. The lack of affect, the lack of memory.

I think the key is not to expect a magic cure-all, but to look for improvement and accept the illness.

Do you find that certain people, places, activities or things hold new meaning for you now or bring you comfort that you never thought about before? How so?

Have a thirty five year diagnosis of bipolar I disorder. Because of that, my comforts and help for others has changed over the years. I have a twenty five year remission of my most manic experiences.

Because my episodes were so beyond the normal, I was caught up in dramas that I created when manic. It was fourteen years before I got a stable grip on it. Because of all that drama, when I became stable I valued stability over all things. I began to feel drawn to the boredom I had rejected as a young man, that of life in society, getting ahead, family life, the humdrum existence of routine.

My attitude now is "give me that boredom and humdrum life." Stability is taking my meds, being a husband of twenty three years and being a grandfather. All the things that once repelled me, I now value as welcome markers in having a fulfilling life. I am grateful for having a second chance. My work as a psychotherapist, my wife, my step-daughters and my grandchildren, they give my life meaning.

Have any of the adjustments you've made produced unexpected consequences or benefits? If so, what are they?

Over the thirty-five years of having mental illness and twenty-five years in recovery, what has helped me most significantly to adjust, was writing and self-disclosing to others. One unexpected consequence of this was the incorporation of mental illness into my persona of who I am. This has caused me to be more open and self-accepting. This certainly wasn't planned or expected. Writing and having articles published in magazines, besides helping my self esteem, caused me to value myself as a person so I am less inclined to stigmatize myself to myself. It's like the old expression, 'When you've got lemons, learn to make lemonade.' Getting my story about mental illness out to others and letting people know you can have a life despite it, serves to reinforce my value as a caring person.

It has unexpected problems at times, of course. There are always the individuals you run into who, after I tell them about my history, view me in a negative manner or want to distance themselves from me. Fortunately, that doesn't happen often. Still, there is always the need to evaluate who you tell your life's story to.

As it relates to mental illness do you continue to learn? If so, in what ways?

I have never stopped learning about myself and my diagnosis. When I started out in recovery twenty five years ago, I didn't know how far I could reach. No one told me and no one knew. Before my mental illness, I thought I wanted a life full of adventure and drama. I wanted to live life on a big screen. When I became mentally ill, it transformed my every moment into drama upon drama, coloring my already dramatic lifestyle. Fourteen years later, after more recovery began to take root; all I wanted was a normal existence, working a job, coming home at night, the possibility of marriage. In short I wanted all of the things I had rejected in my youth. Boredom was good. Life with structure and routine was even better.

The drama I had when mentally ill was so overwhelming, it was preventing normalcy. Now, many years in recovery, I covet my 'boring' life. But the fact is, my life is far from boring. Routine, everyday life is appreciated and valued. Just give me the center of the road, I say. It has been the central truth of my life. Life is interesting in any context when you have your health, especially your mental health. I find that I can stretch. That is, I can do more and more over time if I pace myself and do things in stages. While I may have to be cautious, I can expand my abilities. Whether this knowledge is from age or illness, I can't say. It's probably both.

How has the reality of the illness affected the way you engage and interact with others?

My mental illness was MY BIG secret! Funny thing was, everyone knew! For years I tried to keep my mental illness a secret. I would say things like "I'm just quirky" or "I'm just in a bad mood today." My mental illness manifested itself at a very early age. I guess I was around five years old when I started showing signs of being 'different.' It started with OCD and then came the bipolar behaviors with all that anxiety. At first, my friends and family thought it was bad behavior.'

They couldn't see that I wasn't in control and I didn't want to act differently. I just wanted to be a normal kid. I learned to become a really great liar! I'm forty five now and I've noticed that most people with serious mental illness have had a lot of practice at lying. We lie to our families, clergy, psychiatrists, teachers, lovers, and employers. This is how we are able to blend into the normal world. The lies are not meant to be malicious; rather, they are to protect ourselves from harm. We are REALLY good at them and it takes a skilled professional lots of time to weed out the truth from the lies to help us.

The way that I interact with others now is with great caution. I will tread lightly around the subject of mental illness and let them know that I am an advocate for NAMI and explain about stigma. I will do all of this without 'outing' myself. I will test the waters. If they are receptive, I will let them in slowly. This is even true for my closest friends and family. When dealing with other people with mental illness, I realize that they are scared too. They will lie at first about their illness unless they are in a very safe setting.

Today, I am a motivational speaker talking about my experiences as a person who is mentally 'different.' I stay away from the term 'ill' because I don't feel sick, rather, this is just the way God made me and I am very similar to many people in this world.

I use myself as a platform to reach others and help them to accept themselves and love who God made them to be. I encourage them to take medication to create a better self and learn to have hope for the future. I speak to youth groups, business professionals, law agencies, and any group that wants to learn the truth about what a REAL person with mental illness survives every day...and I am surviving!

What have been your biggest relationship challenges and how have you dealt with them?

New relationships can be explosive! Trying to make a new relationship work can be so difficult for you as a person living with mental illness. It is second nature to lie about yourself to cover up the difficulties that may arise in your new relationship. Trust issues are hard for people living with mental illness. Even learning to talk to therapists and psychiatrists can be tricky. Taking the process slowly and not putting pressure on a new relationship gives me the courage to be honest so I can move forward towards a healthy connection. As a person living with mental illness, my first instinct is to lie and cover up my illness. However, 'it takes a village' and a big part of that village is the person who will be my partner. I'm going to need someone to be my eyes and ears, and my common sense should I be unable to have those things for myself. The closest person to me will be my partner in life and I need to be honest from the beginning. No secrets! That is the best way to help maintain my own healthy state of mind.

8

LIVING & WORKING
WITH MENTAL ILLNESS

I put on a 'work persona' along with my pantyhose each morning.

What do you do for a living, how long have you been at it?

I am an Administrative Assistant. I have been for thirty one years.

I am a Nanny. I have been doing this for about eight years now. It's really kind of ironic because my son was raised by my parents when he was removed from my custody due to the fact that I was dual-diagnosed. He was five at the time. He is now twenty four.

As a student, I've held different jobs, several in retail. Currently I'm working at a small business as office manager. I've been there a year.

How candid can you be about your condition with your boss and those you work with?

At first, I did not say anything. It was really hard because I felt like I was keeping a secret. Then the mother of the child I cared for came to visit from back east and she was the best!

I found out that mental illness runs in her family, so I was able to tell her ALL about myself. She then told her daughter who totally was ok with it. I feel SO much better. I don't feel like I'm hiding something.

Although I never discussed my actual condition with an employer or the people I worked with, at one point, when my symptoms were really bad, it became increasingly difficult to keep it out of the workplace. At the time I was working in retail, and it really started to affect my work performance. When the anxiety got so bad, I had to retreat to the stock room and cry. I wished I didn't have to. I didn't know how I could explain it to my co-workers.

Sometimes I would be so depressed that it became difficult for me to do anything. I would either not show up to work or show up and attempt to avoid my supervisors throughout my entire shift. Eventually my behavior did lead to a couple of discussions with my manager and I decided that it would be better for me to quit that job.

How do you deal with resentment, self-pity and depression – both your own and from others?

My strong faith in God. I also have my family who are Christians and are all praying people. Looking back at dealing with my son's illness, I, as his mother, really helped him get through that rough period. Also, the therapists were a great help.

It's really helped to constantly have the bigger picture in mind. I've been able to eliminate a lot of the self-pity by realizing it's the last thing that will help me accomplish my goals. I've also had to keep in mind the importance "letting go" of people and things that are not conducive to my recovery. I've learned that sometimes you have to put yourself in other people's shoes. Especially in the case of my family, I realize that I have to try to be supportive because my mental illness is not just about me, it affects them as well, positively and negatively.

What behaviors or symptoms caught your attention?

Feeling sad for three weeks at a time. Having a lot of energy, not much sleep, spending more than I should, then regretting it after.

When I felt the feeling of sadness, I would try to get in and see my therapist. Also, calling my good friend would help.

No matter what I do to manage my brain, its not that simple. Sometimes things I hear on the radio make me angry. Breaking the radio doesn't work so well, I have found that changing the station is the better alternative. That and taking my medication.

Once you had acknowledged the condition, what was the most important or positive thing you did to deal with it?

I tried to learn as much as I could about my illness and I'm happy to say that understanding it better really helped me in dealing with it.

I went online, read articles, browsed through books. The more I began to learn why I felt the way I did and what I could do to help myself through it, the more I believed in my own ability to help myself.

What does your daily (or weekly) routine look like?

I like to take a water aerobics class first thing in the morning at the Y. I make sure I have a good breakfast, make a few calls to friends and dress for work. I work three days a week at an antique store about six hours a day. I come home, rest, and read my mail. I talk to my boyfriend, make dinner, watch some television, go to bed.

Luckily, I've been able to incorporate a variety of positive things into my weekly routine. I work full-time during the week, but I've also managed to include a few evenings of volunteer work. When school is in session, I have class on one or two evenings a week, depending on how many classes I'm taking at the time.

On other days I go to the gym - sometimes I enjoy an incredibly fun Zumba class and sometimes I get to spend some time on the treadmill enjoying music on my iPod.

I've found that keeping myself busy with activities that make me feel good about myself has been a very important part in maintaining my emotional stability.

What do you consider to be a "good day"?

Peace and quiet, no drama. No challenges of any kind.

A good day is one that I don't feel like I'm totally abnormal, when I can flow with the day. A really good day is when I don't have to work at not being depressed.

For me, a "good day" begins when I'm able to get out of bed and don't feel like I would do anything to get back in. It's nice when my moods are under control and my irritability doesn't get in the way of my ability to get along with people. It's on those days that I don't have to deal with the rejection of other people wanting to avoid me because they're unsure about how to deal with me. I like when I'm able to be productive and then relax, instead of becoming exhausted and overwhelmed. A good day is topped off when I'm able to follow my bedtime routine, turn on the radio, and gently fall asleep.

What are your proudest moments dealing with mental illness?

My proudest moment was being a counselor, running support groups and speaking to the clients one-on-one, sharing my illness with others and being able to listen to what they were going through and explaining what I had to go through and how I went about it. Helping myself.

Thinking about where I was five years ago, and how far I've come since then makes me proud. Things aren't perfect, but I've certainly come a long way. I'm also proud to be involved with NAMI and everything that we do educate people about mental illness and the support that families have received as a result of NAMI'S efforts.

Can you describe the first time you felt like you had turned the corner towards getting your life under control?

Getting my life under control was a long process over the years. However, the most significant time in which I felt like I had turned a corner towards getting my life under control involved being hospitalized. In 1982, I was making my living making one-of-a-kind lamps and lighting fixtures. My bipolar disorder had been latent for two years, the longest I had ever gone without an episode. This fact I attribute to my working at a creative endeavor. I always had a life-long dream to be an artist. In pursuit of that dream, I had lined up a gallery in the Pacific Design Center, an upscale, premiere outlet for home furnishings open only to the interior design trade. Two weeks before I was scheduled to bring my lamps to the gallery I had a manic episode so severe my dream died stillborn. After that episode I didn't walk into my studio for over a year.

After a year of working in a warehouse, I quit and slept on my mother's couch for months. Finally I regained some sense of hope and began to job hunt again, this time looking to use my degree and experience in psychology. I lined up a job once more but before I could start I had another manic episode and was hospitalized. My greatest fear of being hospitalized in a mental hospital came to pass. My ten-year fear of being locked away for a lifetime, my normalcy about to be unmasked as a hopelessly chronic mental patient, was going to become a fact, or so I perceived it at the time.

That hospitalization taught me my that fears were unfounded. I was in the hospital for two weeks.

Two weeks after discharge, a bit shaky from my recovery, I began to work again at a job I lined up. That was the beginning of a recovery which has lasted over twenty years. I learned that I could survive hospital stays and that it could be a good thing. This whole experience brought home to me the fact I was turning a corner in my life.

There were a few times when I said to myself "Ok, I'm tired of feeling like this. I'm going to take control and finally feel better...for good." The problem was that I was young and never made the commitment to do everything that it took to finally retain some kind of stability, so I would always slip back. It wasn't until I began to think about what I wanted to do with my life and realized that there was a whole lot I hoped to accomplish. I wanted to dedicate my life to educating and helping other people and it was going to take me being healthy to do so. It was when I made a commitment to my own recovery, that I turned that corner, because it was no longer just about me. It was about the difference I hoped to make in the lives of others.

What's the best advice that anyone ever gave you about living with a mental illness?

If you end up on medication and it works don't play games with it by not taking it. You may hold onto that feeling of being OK without it for awhile, but then you crash and crash hard. You can lose ground that may have taken you months to get through. You have to treat medication for any mental disorder like you would medication to control high blood pressure. You need to take it and accept it, or you can die.

⚜

Everybody has something in their life that's not perfect.

⚜

One of the best pieces of advice I got regarding living with a mental illness is to remember that my mental illness is just one part of me, not something that defines my entire existence. It was especially important for me to hear this. For the longest time, I absolutely defined myself by my mental illness and my ability (or failure) to manage it. I let my illness define me and hold me back from believing in myself. I don't let myself do that anymore and it's really unleashed a world of possibilities for me.

Do you find yourself trying to keep up a public façade? If so, why and how do you maintain it?

A small handful of people with whom I work know some of the less savory details of my life. But in order to appear professional, you simply cannot blab everything that is painful or upsetting to the people with whom you work, and certainly not to clients, or to neighbors, or the lady checking my groceries. You can NOT be open about everything in your life to everyone, or you'd spend the day doing nothing but talking about yourself. And frankly, most people have their own lives and their own problems. They're not that interested in my stuff.

I guess I compartmentalize my life. A small handful of trusted confidantes get to know everything. Others get the parts in which they are interested or that are pertinent to them.

Do you know of an example of the resiliency or triumph of the human spirit that came out of dealing with mental illness?

I would have to say that my recovery story is an example of the resiliency and triumph that came out of dealing with mental illness. I have had a mental illness diagnosis for over thirty-five years and have had no episodes for over twenty five years. I owe a lot of this to medication and a good support system. It took over fourteen years for me to start to gain back the normalcy I'd had prior to my illness. I suffered greatly in the first years, getting caught up in delusion and psychosis, taking that in as reality and trying to live in the world that my mind gravitated toward. When I began to try regaining my sanity, my mind balked. I tried working various career jobs, only to be crippled by anxiety. Working jobs was all I could do to attempt regaining my pre-mental illness level of functioning. My biggest fear was that I would not succeed and would live a life which was not only dissatisfying, but a shell of who I had been prior.

However, I persevered for over a decade, moving from one job to the next until I felt strong enough. Strong enough to consider a social life and meeting someone to marry. I was lucky in love. My wife helped provide emotional help which allowed me to return to college and become a therapist. The creative talents I had which had lain dormant for so many years and had withdrawn during the many years of manic episodes began to resurface. Music, writing and singing slowly returned such that I was able to make fuller use of myself as a helper to others and I was able to connect with my emerging psychotherapy practice clients, many of whom were also bipolar.

None of this was easy. For instance, the licensing test for becoming a Marriage and Family Therapist includes an oral exam. I did not pass the first time. In fact, it took me seven tries before I succeeded. The test was only offered two times a year, so it took me four extra years to complete testing to gain my license. I just wasn't going to take no for an answer. Another example of struggling for a life was the way in which I met my wife.

Fourteen years into my illness, I decided I needed to overcome my social anxiety if I was ever to meet someone I could live my life with. I resolved to go out every night of the week to some singles event, seven nights a week until I met someone. I met my wife within three months. Today we have been married twenty-three years. All this as a result of having a major disability and not letting it define your life or who you are. Perhaps others won't have as complete a recovery as I have had. However, I didn't know how far I could reach. You just have to keep trying and not lose hope.

I think that anyone who has experienced mental illness, whether their own or that of a loved one, serves as an example of the resiliency of the human spirit. Mental illness, and all the things that come with it, present us with some of the greatest challenges we could face as human beings. Experiencing mental illness can break us down completely, make us feel depleted and completely lost. However, I truly believe that such experiences can also give us the potential to show what we are capable of as human beings. Looking back, if I hadn't gone through some of the things I went through and overcame, I would have never known I had that kind of strength in me. As painful as living with a mental illness can be, I'm grateful for all the people living with it and all of the families that have been there to support them. It means that there are that many more people who haven't taken life for granted and who will make a difference in the lives of others, whether they realize it or not.

LOSS & GRIEVING

We grieve especially the loss of what could have been.

When you grieve, do you mourn the thing, person or relationship as it was, or do you mourn the dream of what it, they or you might have become? How are those feelings different and which is worse?

I mourn what kind of life my son could have had, reaching his full potential, being fulfilled. I lost my hope for a good life for my son, but also for myself, my husband and grandson. I feel sort of cheated.

⚜

My son took his life at the hand of his bipolar disorder, so my loss is obvious—his whole future being as my son and part of our family, as well as the accomplishments we all saw for his life. He was brilliant (as those bipolar bears all are!) and was going to medical school. Such an awful waste. And we all miss him so much.

He was mostly manic, so seemingly "normal" (even better than normal!), that we questioned his diagnosis. So I didn't feel the loss of "him" until he died. But afterwards, I went to a NAMI meeting, just to see what it was about, and after listening to the pain that the families were going thru…these people were still living with the pain (and much worse) that I had lived with when my son had his break and hospitalization and diagnosis, nine years previously. Some had been living with the constant fear and pain of loving their mentally ill children for decades, some not knowing from day-to-day where they were, or if they were still alive; if they should give them twenty dollars or let them go. Not knowing if they were really helping or enabling. Dare I say aloud that I had a fleeting thought that my dear son had saved me from this life of constant anguish? It sounds horrible, and what he gave me instead is a life of constant sadness for having lost him. And of course I still wish he were here every day. But I'm not sure who is hurt more by this devastation—the people who are ill, or those who love them. I know, it's not a contest.

The support group Survivors After Suicide has helped comfort me and teach me, and I have arrived at a place of acceptance of my son's choice to end his misery. Especially when I hear others share like-stories that I can identify with, and I believe—as he did—that his illness would have worsened over time, especially since he never took any medication. I sadly recognize—as he refused to—that meds might have saved his life, but we'll never know. He's just gone.

Growing up, our daughter was a very confident, feisty child, very independent and outgoing. Her psychotic, depressive episodes have left her insecure, much more introverted and less able to tackle the ups and downs of everyday life. The medications she has to take have made her put on a lot of weight so that she is barely recognizable as the slim, athletic woman she once was. She has totally lost her confidence with members of the opposite sex and her erstwhile boyfriend has since married and moved on with his life, which I know must be a source of ongoing pain for her. She had been in a relationship with him for seven years. They were high school sweethearts.

We grieve especially when we think what could have been. It took us the intervening decade to realize that what we had originally envisioned her life would be will never happen. We feel guilty when we remember that many other victims of mental illness have it so much worse than she does. She is relatively stable and has an emotionally and financially supportive family to act as a safety net for her, but her episodes hang over the whole family like a black cloud that won't permanently go away and we live in dread of it all happening again.

Only people who have gone through something like this can appreciate what a scourge mental illness is and although we are very aware as a family that we have emerged stronger from this, we are not yet at the stage where we can totally accept that all of this was for the best.

Her future is so uncertain. Even with all her accomplishments she has been un-employed for over thirteen months and her current job is only part-time and tempo-rary. We wonder whether she will ever be able to fully support herself again. Probably not. The only thing that helps is to hear other victim's stories and to realize that we're not alone in our ongoing pain. That is why we're participating in this project.

We grieve the loss of the person who was once our daughter and the future that was denied her.

My family basically disowned me, I was alone and on my own, for holidays, etc. I did a lot of growing up in those fifteen years. I know that, for me, it was the best thing they could have done. Sometimes you have to lose the most important thing in your life to realize that.

What caused your loss or what caused your dream, hope or expectation to never be realized?

We all hope to have a so-called normal life. Having had a very difficult abusive childhood, I was never going to have a child, unless I could provide a harmonious setting.

I know that I was a very good caring mother. I also know that my son can get bet-ter if he would get the proper help. He refuses. My husband is also very disappointed. He also just wanted a good life.

How long has it been and what still hurts?

Twenty years. Since the hope of improvement diminishes, I feel very sad, but force myself to go on. I realize that each moment is important and cannot be wasted.

Whom did you lose? How and when did you lose them?

I lost my boyfriend. I had decided it was time to get it together and stopped doing drugs and stayed away from toxic people. My boyfriend lived in another state and wanted to come see me for Christmas. I had a bad foreboding but chose to ignore it. When he got to LA it was great for a day. We went shopping and he bought me a pre-engagement ring but the whole way home was miserable and we began fighting. This kept on for a day. He virtually had me a prisoner in my room while he drank and drank in an empty living room with a sad-looking Charlie Brown Christmas tree.

I was scared. I returned the ring and finally asked him to leave. It was long and torturous, but he finally left at noon on Christmas day. I changed my phone number, returned all gifts he so graciously left for me. I held my breath and kept going. Then I found out a week later he shot himself in the head when he got back home and because I changed my phone number he called my work number and left the sound of the shot on my voicemail. His wires were so crossed and I felt that I was not there to save him. I realized he saved me, but how sad and what a price this revelation has cost.

My mother died of cancer on my tenth birthday. She first became ill when I was about five or six years old, had a radical mastectomy and then radiation treatment. She seemed to be in remission for a few years, though she almost died of pneumonia, and was very ill for the last year of her life. My memories of that time are still rather nightmarish. I was old enough to be aware of much that was going on, but NOT old enough to really process it.

In many ways, it has been good for me. Losing a beloved parent is one of the worst things that can ever happen to anyone, at any age, and I got it out of the way early (wry smile). Later problems, a low grade on a test, a breakup with a boyfriend, scrambling to find rent money, when held up against my personal scale of tragedy, they just weren't as big a deal. So, I was able to cope with things that fluster most adolescents and young adults, with a fair amount of equanimity.

What has been hard has been going through the grieving process. As an adolescent, I found being 'the girl whose mother died' an unwelcome burden, and did what I could to keep friends and teachers from finding out. By pretending I wasn't affected by such a big loss, I couldn't grieve properly. I didn't even start the process till I was almost thirty. Since then, I've done a lot of grief work. I continue to do more as I need it, as milestones come up, or just memories that hurt.

A few months ago, I passed the age my mom was when she died. An age I knew I would never reach - lol! Now, I can think of my mom and enjoy the good memories. Even the bad ones don't hurt quite as much.

I lost the dream of our son growing up and flying free. When our son had his initial breakdown, we imagined it was something that could be overcome, that we would all move beyond, and that would enrich us with the wisdom that suffering can bring. Instead, our son had one breakdown after another.

Each long island of calm between illness became less and less comforting and it became clear this was no simple challenge. Then, finally, he was formally diagnosed with schizophrenia. We were relieved that we knew at last what was happening to him. And then we were consumed with sadness.

We grieved. We questioned. Why our son? Why our family? Hadn't we suffered enough already? Couldn't the bad years and the bad behavior of the past be enough? Other families struggled to raise troublesome teens. Why were we chosen to live on and on in the same trouble. Why did we have to learn this painful lesson? In the early years, our families did not know how to help us. They didn't mean to be so hurtful, but they offered suggestions like, "if only you hadn't been so..." or "If you had just..." They didn't know; we didn't know. Mental illness is not anyone's fault. Our sense of confusion, loss, guilt, was immeasurable. Our son was not yet twenty when he was diagnosed. He still lives with us these many years later, but his future, and our dreams for his future seem lost to us all.

Is there anything else related to loss that you'd like to share?

I've found that other losses seem to echo this great one. Sometimes it is easier/safer to grieve the loss of a pet, though I know when I grieve for a pet, I am also grieving for the BIG loss in my life.

Also, losing a relationship seems to echo back to the big loss, as well. So I have to be careful not to cling to a bad relationship out of fear of loss, of grief, because I've done that and it's never worked well for me.

One thing that is interesting about suicide survivors is how many of us never realized our family member or friend had a mental illness that could lead to their deaths. The statistics are clear, and scary, about the relationship between mental illness and suicide. I think we want so badly to believe that everything will be okay that we miss the signs, or don't make the connection. Even though I pride myself on being very realistic, I guess denial is a very comfortable place to live.

As a person, how were you changed by this loss and your grief? Has your loss substantially changed your identity? If so, how?

There's a reason that Disney bumps off the moms of the characters in or before the first act. Your mom is the person who has got your back, who protects you, who believes in you, no matter what. When you lose your mom as a child, you probably have many experiences, both bad and good, that you would have missed if she had been there.

And, since I'm a woman, that mirror has been missing. The way you compare yourself to your same-sex parent, saying to yourself, "I want to be exactly like her in this and this and that way, and I CERTAINLY don't want to be like her in this, this and that way." Instead of a mirror, you have a big, gaping hole. One that I've been trying to fill, in various ways, all my life. But, this absence also frees you to be creative, to be wilder and more adventurous. I miss her, I always will, but I do think that in many ways I have a strange strength and depth that I would not have had, if she had been present.

There is an underlying sadness to things I experience now. I sometimes wonder if I can ever know real joyfulness again. I used to be the happiest person in the world! Okay, not that I'm never happy. I do know that humor and friends and family are part of the beauty of the world, and I can and do enjoy all of that, almost every day. But when I can't even go to see some animated movie about a panda mom whose son moves away without SOBBING (and no doubt scaring all of the little children in the theatre) when she gives this big speech about losing him, well, it's clear that this loss will just never leave. It's always lurking in the background, ready to pounce. Losing a child is certainly the worst thing in the whole world.

Then, my husband died of a heart attack a year after my son's suicide. I find dating again to be very difficult deciding if or when to expose my sad story. It changes the mood and tenor, and possibilities, of any relationship. One of the very saddest things I had to come to terms with is the reality that whomever I find to (hopefully) spend the rest of my life with, will never have known my son. I cry just thinking about it. God, I hate that! I can never have my boy's memory a shared thing with my lover, even though my son's life and death are among the most important truths of my life. I even dread the pending demise of my last pet dog who knew both my husband and son… It is like her passing will be the last of them. Loss, by whatever means, is a painful, life-changing event. Acceptance is hard-won.

As a result of what you've been through how do you now help others go through grief? What would you say, or not say, to another person going through the same experience now?

I try not to help too much, just lend an ear, rather than trying to fix it/them. To a child, I would say, "I know this feels really awful and scary, but you know your mom still loves you, and always will."

To someone helping a child, I would suggest that they locate peer groups, if possible, of other children who have lost parents, so the child has someone to talk to who 'gets' it. I also highly recommend the book *Motherless Daughter* by Hope Edelman, both for surviving parents to read so they 'get' what their daughter is going through, and as something for the child herself to read, as she nears adulthood.

I would not try to distract the child, or offer a lot of hooey about Mom being an angel or waiting for him or her in heaven. Let the child experience what s/he needs to experience, in her or his own time.

⚜

I would love to share a conversation that I heard on TV that absolutely turned my head around about sharing the loss of a loved one. Two young women were talking in a bar, having met only a short while before, but becoming friends. When one mentioned that she lost her mom, the other did NOT ask how she died (as I usually do, being the concerned, possibly nosy person that I am), but rather, she asked... get this...

"OH, TELL ME ABOUT HER."

I was immediately reduced to tears at the simplicity and the basic truth she hit upon—that all we really want to do, after losing a loved one, is <u>talk about them</u>, who they were, what they did, how wonderful they were, how much we miss them. This thought was magical for me.

Did the loss draw people closer together or push them farther apart?

The loss left me on my own. I had no one to help me hold it together and my so-called friends blamed me. His family members did not want to know me. In my own family, some tried and some didn't try to help me. I had to just tear myself away and isolate and get help.

I joined a group for suicide survivors who helped me in those first few weeks, months, and years. This group was so great and I don't know what I would have done without them. I spent the next three years pretty much sorting it all out and finding who I really was. I got into therapy, began taking the right medication, and slowly made new friends - real friends. It is an ongoing process, building self-esteem and learning to trust others.

I experienced loss when my son was diagnosed with bipolar disorder. Also the loss of friends who just didn't understand or were scared of it. They kept their distance, so I learned to be a little more discerning about sharing the information. My close family was great, even though my dad had a hard time. He was a US Marine who thought any bad behavior could be fixed with a kick in the ass. He didn't hold much with psychological stuff, therapy either. But he, and my mom and sister and her family, still kept close, and best of all, aren't afraid to bring up his name or tell stories about him.

Then there is his brother, who wants nothing to do with any of it. When the diagnosis was made nine years ago, he pulled away from anything to do with it. He may not even have believed it, since he says he suffered abuse and bullying at this brother's hand when they were young. He adored his older brother so this had to be painful. Now, he has gone through so much loss himself (father, brother, step-father) that he is obviously really angry, and will not "talk about sad things," as he says, or be close to me. I worry a lot about his repressed feelings, and can only hope for the best for him. A wise therapist told me that the reason a lot of boys/young men do not attend support groups or get therapy (or help of any kind) is that, in their twenties and thirties, all of their emotional energy is being used for gaining independence, and they just don't have it to give over to healing their emotional wounds. So they are "saving" it for a time when they can afford emotionally to do it. That sounds really right to me. Let's hope so, because I want to be close to him again. Having lost one son is hard enough, ya know?

Was there anything that could have prepared you for the loss?

My son was diagnosed with bipolar disorder at sixteen when his behavior at school became erratic and we discovered his drug and alcohol use that he used to self-medicate. He was at the peak of a perfect junior year. Academic decathlon, straight A's, starring in the school play, championship swimmer. He was doing the kind of work I always knew he could do. He was brilliant, charming, and gorgeous.

His bad behavior was scary although just a little worse than what we heard all of our friends say about all of their kids. He ran away, I caught him taking some painkillers from the medicine cabinet, then we went to the hospital. He was diagnosed in twenty minutes, and spent three-and-a-half weeks in the adolescent unit with other kids who had attempted suicide. We didn't know that he had attempted a year before. He was a great patient, running the group therapy sessions and really helping the other kids - the doctor said he should be a psychiatrist.

When he came home, he was clean, working and going to school part-time. Three years later, his father and I split up, and he and his younger brother stayed with me. Then we had a fight over girls and alcohol and drugs, none of which were part of our living arrangement, and he left the house for nine months. It was the scariest time of my life. I didn't know where or how he was doing for weeks at a time, only that he was angry with me.

When he finally returned home, I was remarried and E went to school seriously and tutored to pay his expenses. He became engaged to a lovely girl, graduated cum laude, traveled to Taiwan to teach English, and was just wonderful in every way. My family and I talked about how he must have been misdiagnosed. He was choosing between Harvard and U. of Singapore for medical school. We had parties with his friends, and wonderful debates about politics and religion. Then my son killed himself - after five wonderful years. He was twenty five.

My family was devastated. All of the usual questions were asked - how, where, but mostly, why. How could he when he had so much to look forward to?

But my son gave us an awesome gift along with his awful death. He had a blog - akumaprime.com - where he recorded his travels and thoughts. And where he explained why he chose suicide. He told us how much pain he was in, that his brain was 'on fire.' He explained that it was no more a selfish thing to take his life, than it was for us to ask him to stay alive for us.

Of course I was hurt and angry and frustrated, all the gamut of feelings you would expect. But my son relieved me of any guilt or ignorance.

The one thing I still beat myself up about is that I didn't see that he was, at twenty five years old, going through the same high peak experiences that I saw in high school, when he had the first break. I had a little flash of recognition, a little "Uh oh, this reminds me of his junior year...", but I didn't get the alert. I don't know what I think I could have done. Nothing, really. He was determined, had planned it for almost a year.

Still, you keep on wishing, and thinking, "If only..."

What are your biggest regrets dealing with mental illness?

My biggest regret was not knowing or realizing my daughter's behavior was due to mental illness. For many years, I believed she was a 'flake' for not following through on job and family commitments. I couldn't understand her behavior.

I wish I knew more about mental illness, and symptons of my illness.

I kept hoping that my son would take his illness seriously and keep going for a therapist and take the medications. I should have been firm and given ultimatums. I did not deal with it properly.

I regret that I was not available to help my loved one when he first became ill. He was hospitalized for depression at age sixteen for six weeks. He received little or no treatment for twenty-five years, when he finally allowed his family into his home, which was ruined. It was filled with trash, dog mess, and furniture turned sideways and stacked to the ceiling. In summary, it should have been condemned.

I regret that I didn't donate his body to science after he died. I wish someone had said something to me. His brain may have held significant evidence for study and possible help for scientific research.

What do you wish you had done or not done in getting to a diagnosis and seeking help for your child?

I wish that I had believed the diagnosis. I didn't really want to believe it, so every time there was any evidence that my son was doing well, I jumped at the chance to believe he was misdiagnosed. Friends told me that bipolar disorder was being over-diagnosed at the facility my son went to in particular, as well as just in general.

But I read Danielle Steele's book about her son (in addition to every book I could find on the subject) and every detail of her description of her son was identical to my son. Her son killed himself. Why would I refute this comparison and its obvious implication of the death threat awaiting my son?

He suffered his breakdown and was diagnosed in his junior year of high school, at a time when he was at the top of his game - in a major manic phase. One guilty moment I have agonized over happened in retrospect, after his death, when I realized that I had seen him experiencing that same 'top of his game' phenomenon right before his suicide. Oh, how I wish I had recognized the sheer mania of that time so that I could have said or done something important enough to him to change his mind. It still brings tears to my eyes to reflect on that painful truth, and I can forgive myself that fatal mistake, with this unavoidable truth: I believe absolutely that, had I been able to prevent my son's death, there would eventually have been another time when he would have succeeded.

In hindsight is there anything you wish you would have spotted or acted upon sooner?

I wish that I had insisted that my son seek help at once and made sure he took his medication once he got help. But it was not consistent and the situation was very different then. He functioned.

He never took any medication after hospitalization, saying that the only thing he learned there was how to bring a pill up (from his sternum). I failed to understand the ramifications of his not taking meds. I didn't know how to force him to take them (or to do anything, really), but I didn't try very hard. I was thinking he was so smart, he knew himself, was in charge of himself. I was fooled over and over again by how great he was doing. I just totally missed the boat.

What or who are the most important resources for dealing with mental illness and loss?

The two best resources that helped me deal with my son's bipolar disorder are:

1. BILY (Because I Love You), a kind of tough love group that is an advocate for the parents and the family of troubled teens. While not specifically for mental health issues, they provided great information and real down-to-earth, practical help for the daily logistics of living with kids that challenge the whole family unit. It was comforting and encouraging to hear the experiences of others who had been through what we were going through. And I was amazed at what great ideas they had for coping with the seemingly unsolvable problems caused by kids run amok (for whatever reason). I had a son whom I adored and hurt for every day, and yet had to protect myself from to get through his volatile teenage years.
2. Because my son did eventually take his life at twenty five, I found a group called SAS (Survivors After Suicide), and believe me, I know how much you are praying even as you read this, that you will NEVER need to join such a group. But as you know, I'm sure, it is really not in our control, and despite our best efforts, life and death happen. The wisdom and comfort that this group provides to anyone who has lost someone to suicide is remarkable.

SAS helped me in my healing from this MOST heart-breaking loss of my life, dealing with my personal pain, grief, and anger, as well as addressing the embarrassment so many of us feel when facing the stigma attached to suicide.

Most importantly, it is a place to express all of the pain, so you can start to heal and finally come to an understanding and acceptance of what this journey can mean in your life. I learned to place this tragic event in a soft, faraway place in my history, while keeping my son's memory alive for me every day. I find I can look both forward and back with openness and acceptance. Well, maybe not EVERY day, but most.

How did you find out? What was your first reaction?

I'll share that night, never written down before…

My husband and I had just come home from the movies, and were up in our room, watching some TV before bed, when his son came up and knocked at the door. I heard them talking under their breath and I started to join in, then thought better of it. Maybe it was guy stuff, so I let them go off to talk together.

When M returned a few minutes later, he came to my side of the bed and knelt down, taking both of my hands in his,

"What's wrong?" I asked, alarmed.

"There's been an accident. It's E."

He squeezed my hands tightly.

I asked, "But he's okay, right?"

M shook his head, with as much pain on a face as I had ever seen in my life.

"But he's alive, right?" I insisted.

M shook his head again, "No."

And I ran screaming from the room, tearing down the stairs to see my beautiful son's body lying breathless in his bed. I kissed him and held him, caressed his face, pounded on his chest, sobbing, "No, no, no, no, no, no no…" a thousand times, until I was all cried out.

We answered the questions of firemen and paramedics. We found the short note that Evan had left. Later we read in his blog about the pain he could no longer endure.

Can you even imagine the phone call to my parents, having to tell them their grandson was dead…? Or my younger son, that his brother had killed himself or my sister, her beloved nephew? I truly don't know how I did it. I don't remember the calls, except my mother's loud gasp, then whispers to my father. My sister, out of town, got on a plane that hour. My son flew home from college. E's and my closest friends gathered, all of us incredulous, confused, sorrowful.

I never lied about my son's suicide, refusing to feel any shame or guilt. I certainly went through days and weeks of, "If only…"s. But somehow I was able to forgive him.

His eloquent explanation made it seem more like euthanasia, like a suffering puppy that had put himself out of his own misery.

My family and I forged onward together. I thank God every day that I had my husband and his strength and love to get me through the days and months before he too left me, with a sudden heart attack.

Many things play into surviving that much loss. Certainly my faith, my wonderful family and friends, all of whom surrounded me. And I found a new recovery/support group. SAS (Survivors After Suicide) that provided some deep healing that I could only experience with others who have been through this same kind of loss, and felt these same feelings of anger and pain. We help each other when we share our realities.

My son was living with incurable pain and he chose not to live with it any longer. It doesn't really matter whether he was right or not – reality is perception, and he was very sure of his own truth. I miss him, wish he had chosen differently, but he insisted on taking what was rightfully his and he suffers no more.

My Son's epitaph:
Peace and freedom pour down like rain,
Dousing fire in unsound brain.
Brilliant cybernaut, travel through time,
Our beautiful son, The AkumAPRIME

After a difficult loss how have you allowed yourself to invest emotionally again in something else which you might also lose?

After the grief and the loss at first I didn't think we would invest emotionally in anything or anybody ever again. Nevertheless my husband and I didn't want to acknowledge how much our family had been impacted by our daughter's illness and so we decided (once the initial trauma was over) to proceed with our own lives as we had planned. We were lucky that we could do this because she was well enough to be at home alone when necessary.

As it turned out it was a real miracle that we made that decision. Not only did it contribute to her healing because it helped her regain confidence in her ability to function on her own, but also, it let us take advantage of what would subsequently prove to be my husband's last remaining healthy years. About four years after our daughter's breakdown my husband was diagnosed with Alzheimer's disease. His diagnosis led us to decide to do as many of the adventurous things that we wanted to do as quickly as we could before the inevitable neurological deterioration took place.

So we've had five fun years. Our daughter has joined in some of our adventures. (That's one advantage of being unemployed!) We decided to live dangerously and we won. Our daughter has made a lot of progress with her illness. She is relatively stable and has put those years since her breakdown to good use. Living safe is not an option any more. The illnesses of our daughter and my husband have made us all realize how important it is to live each day to the fullest and let tomorrow take care of itself.

ACCEPTANCE

Acceptance can only come from a safe place.
It wasn't until I felt safe enough to tell others I had a mental illness that
I spoke up.

What helped you move from acknowledgement to acceptance? Can you describe any stages in that process?

Years passed before I began to realize that many of the students in the graduate school where I am an administrator were also dealing with mental health issues but most, if not all, did not feel comfortable talking about it.

Once I realized that the depression was an integral part of my life I began to read anything I could get my hands on, to learn more about the disorder. I read and read, but never really discussed it with anyone else. For several years I thought of depression as a small part of who I was, not realizing how very much it would impact my life.

It was then that I decided to begin speaking publicly about my depression in the hopes that by talking about it I could create a safe environment for others to do the same. By sharing my experience with depression and teaching about it in our pastoral counseling class, I began to further clarify for myself exactly what relationship I had with the disease.

Talking about it to others made it more and more real and that helped me accept that the depression would be with me for a lifetime, no different than someone who has diabetes or asthma. It wouldn't necessarily surface on a daily basis and it might remain "silent" for long stretches of time, but it was still a key part of my make-up. I realized that I could fight that or accept that. By accepting it I could learn how to live a productive and fulfilling life with it.

I have to be honest and say that I have yet to fully accept my illness. It's not to say that I'm not working on keeping all my symptoms under control, but there are times that I try to push it away and not accept it as part of who I am. I still have a whole lot of work to do, but I am most definitely making progress. I think that one of the most important steps in the process is making sure to surround yourself with people who are willing to help you in the journey toward acceptance by supporting you and learning about the illness with you, instead of pretending it doesn't exist. Support from friends, family, and everyone I've met in NAMI have really made all the difference in taking big steps in the positive direction.

What's the difference between acknowledging mental illness and accepting it?

The bipolar me was sleeping with men and women. I was totally out of control. I was spending $40,000 and heading right into bankruptcy. Something had to stop this madness. Then I had a psychotic break and ended up in the hospital. When I was told what my diagnosis was, I was so happy. All those years of strange thoughts and behaviors…I finally had a name to call this madness.

I began having 'different' thoughts and behaviors at the early age of five. I felt panicky. I obsessed over everything. I prayed about fear of death. I knew that something was wrong with me. So, when after a battery of tests and years of psychotherapy, they gave me the diagnosis of bipolar with OCD and anxiety, I was relieved. They told me that there were medications. They could try to help me! I couldn't believe what I was hearing. Then, the fear rolled in. What would I tell people. How would this effect my job, my family and relationships? I did what I had to do - I lied. I said I had chronic fatigue syndrome and that I was really under a lot of stress. Of course my family knew better. They knew me all my life and I was in my twenties trying to minimize my mental illness to them. I was acknowledging my mental illness but was not ready to accept it.

Acceptance can only come from a safe place. It wasn't until I felt safe enough to tell people that I had a mental illness, that I spoke up. I was sitting in the waiting room at the psychiatrist's office and a woman there began to talk to me. She told me about NAMI and was very open about her schizophrenia. I was so impressed and felt so safe talking to her that when we finished. I called my best friend to tell her about my illness and we ended up talking for hours. Acceptance is a slow process because we don't know exactly how people are going to react. I may accept my condition one day and then someone close to me may make me feel ashamed or unsafe and I may fall back into trying to minimize it. It's a slippery slope and its a team effort by all who know me.

What or who has the biggest influence on how you see yourself and how you live your life? Why is it significant?

While there are people who are very important, who I trust to have all four wheels on the ground, I've learned to start trusting myself again. I'd picked up distorted thinking from living with someone with mental illness, and as I have built better boundaries and gotten in touch with ME again, I find that I like me. I can trust me.

Outside of myself, I trust my adult son, my immediate boss at work, a dear friend, and one of my sisters. These are all people who would tell me if my brain were getting off-kilter in a serious way.

I really don't know where I would be without my mother. She is the one that has always told me that everything happens for a reason. She taught me that I should embrace my illness as a tool I've been given by the Universe to accomplish my goal of going out in the world and helping other people. "What advice would we be able to give to others if we never went through anything ourselves?" she would say. "How would we ever learn?"

She reminds me that even my most negative experiences should be taken as opportunities to learn and make myself a better person. She also constantly reminds me that even though there are things I still struggle with from time to time, I have come a long way in recovering and it's something I really need to be proud of.

What are your goals, dreams and expectations now and how are they different from before the onset of this condition?

I haven't given up on anything, but I have had to concede that my progress on the things I want to do is going to be much slower than I would have liked. Some things I expected to take priority are on the back burner for now, while I deal with personal issues. And that's okay. Everything really important to me will still get done eventually.

Some of my goals are now very personal, having to do with being mindful, being in touch with my thoughts and feelings and dreams, instead of plunging full steam ahead, and figuring it out along the way. I'm trying to slow down and really decide what I want, rather than grabbing what most appeals to me along the way.

These days, nothing makes me happier than thinking about all the goals and the BIG dreams I have for myself. The fact that I've finally been able to get to the point where I believe in myself and trust myself to plan for my future is exhilarating. It's crazy to think that I used to dread even just waking up in the morning, having to trudge through another day. Now, I get so excited planning out the coming weeks, months, and year. I'm planning on applying to graduate school next year. I'm going to end up being not only the first person in my family to go to college, but first to earn a Master's degree and eventually a doctorate. I'm taking it all the way!

As a person, how have you changed? How have you grown?

I think I'm better, wiser, deeper and sadder, somewhat emotionally and mentally bruised, but also more aware of joy. Had I been given the choice, I would have skipped being involved with someone mentally ill. But if I had managed to do so, I recognize that I would have missed out on so much, so much pain, true, but so much joy. These along with so much hard work, frustration, and acceptance of the unacceptable.

I was reading somewhere that somebody read a comment on people with mental illness, that they should just stop feeling sorry for themselves and go play with their dogs. My own attitude, while not exactly the same, was once not too far off from that.

I can recognize how very hard those with mental illness work to get well, to maintain wellness, how very frustrated they are when their faulty wiring sends them into a tailspin.

Overall, I'm glad I've had this experience. But I feel ready to embrace other experiences, like winning the lottery.

I really am a believer in everything happening for a reason. As much as I've struggled with my mental illness and everything that comes with it, I really do believe that I was meant to go through it all so that I can learn, grow as a person, and eventually use all of that to help other people. At twenty-something, I'm grateful that I've learned a bit about what it takes to cope when things become incredibly overwhelming and you can't even seem to get your own thoughts straight. I've learned to be a better listener, because I now know how crucial it is to have someone who truly listens to you. It makes all the difference. I've been able to use all this to help my friends and to teach them how to be there for people they love.

Has this condition brought you into new relationships or friendships, and if so, how and with whom?

Because I've had to do so much legwork to research this on my own, I've come into contact with many different people on support and chat boards I never would have come across in my regular life. Like people everywhere, some are fabulous, and some are okay, and some... I don't know about. But the ones who are fabulous have helped me learn and grow so much as a person dealing with loved one(s) who have mental illness. I've even met a few in person!

I have to be careful to not see everyone through bipolar-tinted glasses. I see it everywhere, as a result of living with my bipolar son and husband, and all of the research I've done, all of the people I've met on the journey. It feels condescending—and wrong—to be a "diagnoser."

Also, being back in the dating game, I meet a "wired" guy and question why I am attracted to that kind of energy. Am I willing or ready to sign up for that again?

The first time I developed new friendships because of my illness was when I was in the hospital for a few days recovering from a severe depressive episode. I still believe that one of the main things that helped me begin to feel better was being surrounded by and getting to talk to other people who knew exactly what I was going through.

I didn't have to explain myself to them and we could all be ourselves and discuss what was really going on inside our heads without worrying that we were going to be judged. I felt so safe. It's similar to what I've experienced with my involvement in NAMI. I'm able to tell my story and hear other people's stories and know that not only am I not alone, neither is my family.

How has the reality of the illness affected the way you engage and interact with others?

In some ways I'm more open, in others I am more wary. I am much more open to talking to others about mental illness issues—and have been surprised at how much is 'out there' in various flavors. At such time as I may consider dating again, I am going to be VERY wary of meeting partners who seem 'too good' on the surface.

Also, during the time I lived with a mentally ill partner, it severely cramped my style—we could only rarely have friends over. Going out in public was always risky due to unpredictible behavior. It was severely limiting. It was difficult at work, too. I work in a small firm where most people are very friendly, and there are several occasions each year when partners are invited to functions.

I always felt like I was walking on eggshells there. While I did not want to discuss my partner's possible mental illness, I also felt that any aberrant behavior of his during events would reflect badly on me at work if I did not. Since I 'came out,' the reaction has been warmly supportive.

I've learned that I have to be patient with other people. As much as you would love for everyone you interact with to be understanding and be sensitive your particular situation, it isn't always possible. I've had to begin to accept that not everyone knows how to deal with some things that come along with mental illness.

I can't be angry about it, because it's not their fault. I've had to learn that it's not appropriate to take out frustrations about what you're dealing with on innocent bystanders (like family). I try to really work on controlling my emotions to avoid conflict and hurting other people's feelings.

What do you know today that you wish you had known on the day your child was diagnosed?

Today, as I look back on the journey so far, I know the road will be long and there will be no end to living with mental illness.

When our son's doctor first called us to suggest "your son may have schizophrenia," we knew schizophrenia as a worst-possible mental illness, but we knew little else. We knew enough to be heartbroken. We started right away to learn as much as we could about his illness so we would be able to help him while we stumbled along, wondering where to place ourselves in this changed-forever world. It has been an exhausting journey, but we learned many things along the way.

We learned how strong we were, how resourceful, how courageous each of us were. We fought for and against one another, but more than anything else, we fought to save our son. We got him the help he needed. We have not yet gotten him to accept help willingly, but we have come to understand that it is his illness that stands in the way. His illness speaks in many ways and we have come to understand some of the language of his suffering.

Some of the lessons we learned were unique to our family and cultural heritage. Shame and ignorance have been difficult to overcome. But we have made progress in enlightening family members who had no previous understanding of mental illness. And we have enjoyed their support as they learned to accept the new shape and texture of our family.

The most valuable thing we learned was not easy to accept. The one thing that we learned and wish we had known all along was this:

"This is the life you live, accept it for what it is, come to terms with it, and live it."

We grieved so deeply and so long for all we had lost, dreams and hopes for our son, dreams and hopes for ourselves. We felt stricken by the limitations that mental illness so clearly placed on us all.

We have finally begun to accept that no matter what our hopes or dreams may have been, it is not for us to decide what life our son should lead. We have begun work towards acceptance of his life as appropriate to him, and try to offer him the simple gifts of acceptance, of trust. We work to understand that there is a lesson to be learned in each day whether that day includes small steps forward or frightening forays back towards the bleak, bad days. All of these lessons are offered to us as an opportunity to learn, to take value, to share. We are humbled by the power of this illness.

What changes did you have to make in your habits, lifestyle, schedule and expectations as a result of the mental illness?

Our son is nearly thirty years old. Our marriage is strong. We find ways to enjoy one another, but we have had to make changes to how we live and what we expect out of life as caregivers. Most of those changes are not good.

We are constantly worried about dying. We are worried that our son will not manage himself well. We know that he will manage well enough when he has to. We know that some people think we should just kick him out and let him fend for himself. We can't do that. We tried, but he just came back, broke into the house and settled back in.

We know that it is helpful and a comfort to him to continue living with us. At least he takes his medication sometimes, sees his doctor, and bathes. Small things. But he has been so sick for so long that even these small things are big accomplishments.

As it is, he has to be reminded to take his medication. He rarely takes it if not reminded. He has to be reminded to eat, or when he is manic and eating wildly, needs to be reminded to eat food instead of just chips and soda. He does not brush his teeth, his room is swimming in dust, he wears the same clothes day after day. He does wash them, and bathes, and that's good but he wears the same clothes, refuses to buy new ones, refuses new clothes we buy for him. He does not leave the house unless he is manic and then he goes back and forth to to the store to buy chips and soda. He refuses all offers to go out. Besides that, he goes only to his monthly doctor's appointment where he spends his time telling the doctor that he does not need medication.

We do our best to be home every evening by ten pm to offer his medication. We go out to dinner only occasionally because we feel so guilty leaving our son home alone. He is always alone - when we go to work, when we go to the grocery store, when we go for a walk. He stays home alone and will not leave the house. We have stopped going to movies and concerts and instead watch movies and concerts on DVD hoping he will watch with us, hoping he will engage in some way with the world outside of our home.

We know there is hope that this can all change for the better, but our life as caregivers is not much of a life right now. We love our son, we love one another, but we would love to have a more joyful life.

One of the most important things I learned about managing bipolar disorder was how crucial it was to really focus on maintaining good habits (eating right, sleeping, exercising) and staying on a schedule. They are all things we should all try to keep in check as it is, but it's especially important you're already prone to extreme mood swings.

The problem is, it's hard to really stick to any of it when you're in college and never seem able to get your three meals a day. You stay up all night studying for exams, and on weekends you want

to join your friends at parties. If I was to focus on managing my symptoms, I was going to have to do the opposite of what most of my peers were doing. I wasn't always willing to. I knew it wasn't good for me, but I didn't think it was fair that I couldn't be a "regular" young adult.

It was only after graduating and coming back home that I was able to find some kind of day-to-day stability. I've been able to maintain a schedule that allows me to plan for the gym and take the time to buy groceries for myself to make sure I'm eating right. My sleep is now more regular more often. Naturally, I DO feel better. Wish I hadn't been so stubborn before.

Was the realization that you were dealing with mental illness sudden and traumatic or a slow evolution?

I have three mentally ill people in my life, and with each I experienced this process differently. The first person I had to deal with was my husband, who is bipolar. I'm a college graduate, but I never took an abnormal psychology class, and, although I had heard of schizophrenia, I had never heard the term manic- depression or, as it's now known, bipolar disorder.

We had been married two or three years when one day I was watching a TV talk show, sometime in the 1980s, on which they were discussing the symptoms of manic-depression…and suddenly a light switch clicked on for me. I thought, "Wow, that sounds just like my husband!"

Once that happened, I was able to start talking to him about getting help. What happened after that is another story … I experienced a lot of resistance to this di-agnosis, not only from my husband but also from mental health professionals, church counselors, and others, because he has milder symptoms than many. That doesn't make the illness any easier to live with, but it does make it more difficult to convince the person that medication might actually be a good idea.

I sometimes wonder why it had to happen to me and my family, but I'm also the parent of two mentally ill adults. I have three children, and when my middle child, a daughter, was eighteen, she came home and told me she needed help. She had been living with her boyfriend for a few months, had quit going to high school, and, come to find out, had been using crystal meth. When I spoke to her that night, she told me she thought she was going crazy, and I asked her if she was hearing voices. She said, "Yes", so I immediately took her to the hospital.

At the hospital she was having difficulty speaking and answering the doctor's questions. The drug screen showed use of amphetamines and marijuana, and they suspected that she was experiencing an overdose. She was hospitalized for a week, and at the end of it, the assumption was that it wasn't mental illness, but the drugs that had caused the episode. I took their word for it. However, when I took her to a drug and alcohol counselor a few days later, the counselor's words to me were, "She's presenting as if she still has residual mental health issues."

After that, it took several months of really bad behavior on her part, being in and out of our home, two additional hospitalizations, and some tough love from me, in order to get her to the point of being willing to take medication. Once she did, however, she was stable enough to come home. Her diagnosis is paranoid schizophrenia, and she is currently stable, but unable to go to school or keep a job. My daughter's diagnosis occurred in 2005.

In 2007, at age seventeen, my son, who had been planning to enter the Marines after high school, was diagnosed with an eye disease that prevented him from entering the military, and essentially makes him legally blind. After that, he spiraled down into a world of depression and heavy use of marijuana.

What kills me is the drug use. Having to experience it with two children made me wonder what I did wrong as a parent. And yet, my husband and I are not drinkers and we don't keep alcohol in the house. We have never been drug users. Sadly, it seems easy for teens and young adults to fall into these patterns of behavior, even when they have seen a completely different example from their parents.

Then, in 2010, my son's disability (SSI) was approved, and he received a lump sum in back payments, which he promptly proceeded to party with. Again, it seems that drug use (he states it was primarily marijuana) precipitated a psychotic break. He began exhibiting symptoms of bipolar disorder, but much worse than I had ever seen in my husband. It became apparent to me very quickly that this was the problem, and I began to try to get him help.

However, in California the standard for hospitalization is high. We had the police come out to our home one time and they refused to take my son, because they must judge the person to be a danger to himself, a danger to others, or severely disabled, and in their minds he did not fit the criteria. However, a few days later, after he was stopped by the police in the middle of the night for driving our car without a driver's license (never mind that he is legally blind), we finally were able to talk him into going into the hospital voluntarily for an evaluation.

Again, it took more bad behavior, two more back-to-back hospitalizations, and much stronger medications in order to get my son stabilized enough to bring home. The process with my son went much more quickly, several weeks, rather than the several months it took with my daughter, partly because she was more defiant and partly because we knew the system better and knew what to expect. My son is now medication-compliant and is working with his psychiatrist in order to fine-tune the medications. If a procedure ever comes along that will help his eyesight, I have great hope for him to live a normal life.

If I were to give advice to someone who might be experiencing the psychotic symptoms of a loved one for the first time, it would be to persevere. Each time I went through this with my adult children, it took multiple visits to the psychiatric ward, and me telling the kids that if they didn't take medication, they could NOT come home (tough love) before we got to the point of some stability.

What it meant was that I had to revise my expectations for my kids. I had to learn to accept some occasionally erratic behavior on the part of my husband and I had to learn to be tough and use whatever leverage I could in order to get them the help they needed. It's not easy, but there is peace in my home now, and that is something!

LEARNING & COMMUNICATING

Learning how to best communicate with your loved one is so important.

What are the best books you have read on the subject? How have they helped you?

I read a diet book called *Potatoes not Prozac*. It was a typical diet book in motivational format. It caught my eye because I took Prozac. It focused on the need to incorporate complex carbohydrate and eliminate simple sugars. I was already a whole multi-grain cereal fanatic so I decided to try out the diet.

I found that by eliminating sugar I had less mood swings.

The book *Brainlock*. It explained how to deal with Obsessive Complusive Disorder (OCD), thereby giving hope that if my son would face his situation and had a desire to, he could improve. He lives a very difficult, secluded life. He is just existing.

Learn as much as you can about mental illness. Read *I Am Not Sick, I Don't Need Help* by Xavier Francisco Amador and *An Unquiet Mind: A Memoir of Moods and Madness* by Kay Redfield Jamison. Join your local NAMI affiliate and start attending a weekly support group. The support groups should help you find local treatment providers. Sign up and attend **Family to Family** classes as soon as possible.

It sounds silly to suggest a book by a novelist, but Danielle Steel's book, "*His Bright Light*" opened my eyes to recognizing bipolar behaviors in my son. It was really valuable to us.

Bebe Moore Campbell's "*72 Hour Hold*" painted a picture of the mental health system, and offered us a sense that we were not alone in this frightening journey. Elyn Saks "*The Center Cannot Hold*" gave us a look into the experience of someone living with schizophrenia.

I'm reading a book on laughter as medicine. I find humor really helps my depression.

Have you found any communication methods or strategies particularly helpful?

I've gotten some of Dr. Xavier Amador's books and have been using the LEAP method, which seems to work well at most times.

Building better boundaries has been ESSENTIAL. At first, I did not recognize that we were dealing with a mental disorder, and I would give in, thinking that this would make my partner feel more secure, or that he would eventually work through his grief/pain/distrust and other issues. Instead, both the situation and my thinking became disordered. You have to stand your ground, not 'let the loonies run the asylum,' as it were, though it is still important to listen to what they have to say and take that into consideration.

The point about boundaries is that once you draw that line, there can be no crossing it, even if on reconsideration you think it's a dumb one after all. You have to defend your turf each and every time there's a boundary violation, or it will keep occurring. Think of a child throwing a tantrum in the grocery store. You can NOT cave in and buy that box of sugary cereal, unless you want the same battle every single time you go in. Your partner needs to learn that you are serious and mean it when you set a boundary. If you are not certain that you can hold the line on a certain boundary, better not to announce a boundary at all than to set one and then cave in.

Learning how to best communicate with your loved one is so important. Be persistent with service providers and do not be afraid to escalate matters with them--including physicians—with the permission of your loved one (or without it if you feel it is necessary). If you do not like the people treating your loved one, and are not getting results, keep looking.

Also, do not underestimate the bond between your loved one and his or her therapist. Therapists are trained to build trust with your loved one and may cut you out of communication unless you have written consent from your loved one, which is often very difficult to obtain. You may have to accept this, even if you feel your loved one is not progressing in their recovery with their current therapist. Your NAMI support group may have suggestions about how to get your loved one to make a change.

SUPPORT & SELF-CARE

*Get educated, join NAMI and read and absorb everything
regarding the situation.*

What advice would you give to a family encountering mental illness for the first time?

Become educated. Join a support group. Knowledge helps to drive out fear. When you realize you are not alone, you will find yourself functioning better. It is so important that the all of the family members take advantage of the help available, particularly through NAMI. There are support groups for the parents, the siblings, spouses and grandparents. The more you know the easier it will be for the family to function.

What's the most encouraging illustration of support for the mentally ill that you know about?

I wholly suggest and advocate medication and therapy. Many people do not want medication but it has helped me to get myself going. Joining support groups, as well as individual therapy and the desire to have things in your life work are the best tools I know of to be able to manage on a day-to-day level. Wanting to be okay and taking the actual steps, hard as they may be, are an integral part of becoming a better 'you', at least they were in my case. That, and having a therapist who is just the best. She helps me to move along and does not make me feel bad for any setbacks that occur. I also have a great husband who is very supportive and understanding. I surround myself with people who really do care and limit or have gotten rid of those who are toxic to me.

Awareness, and people learning that it is not an illness created by the mentally ill - it was not his or her choice. We have to be informed about the facts, it is a medical condition referred to as a brain disorder.

I know that UCLA has a very successful OCD program. I know that with the proper care and medication, many people live very fulfilling lives. In that respect it proves that life is worth it and there is hope for everybody for a better quality of life. In my personal experience, meeting so many interesting people has added a lot to my life. So even when things do not feel so, there are many plus sides. Many people that I know turn their dilemmas into something positive and thereby help others.

Did you know about mental health support organizations before the diagnosis of mental illness? If you learned about them after a diagnosis, how long after?

I didn't know about any support organizations for the mentally ill until our daughter became so ill that she decided she had to see a doctor. This was probably eight months after the initial psychotic break.

I went with her and the doctor gave me the address and telephone number of the local chapter of NAMI. I attended their meetings on my own and heard some wonderful speakers who dealt with the practicalities of having a mentally ill family member. I also heard doctors who specialized in disorders like our daughter has and, best of all,

I heard the stories of countless other family members who were dealing with similar illness in their family.

Oh, how good it felt to know there were other people out there dealing with the same crises as we were and were so full of helpful advice from their own experience. Attending the NAMI meetings gave me new and valuable insight into mental illness and how to cope. I shall be forever thankful to NAMI and will try to advocate for the mentally ill and to support the organization as much as I can financially.

I went to a NAMI meeting after my son took his life, thinking that I could help others to not lose their loved ones, that they could learn from my unfortunate situation. I wound up getting more than I gave.

How did you first hear about NAMI (or support organizations like NAMI)?

When my wife took her life, I knew two things: that I couldn't survive alone, and that I felt a great deal of personal guilt. With no immediate family in the area to turn to, I researched the internet and phone books trying to find support for those who had lost someone to suicide. That's how I found the Survivors After Suicide program conducted by Didi Hirsch Mental health organization, which has been a great help and support to me.

I was frantic and fearful. We did not understand our daughter's behavior. What would happen if we weren't around? Who would help her?

I made an appointment to see a therapist at Kaiser. The therapist who did the intake assessment asked me if I had heard about NAMI. She suggested I check it out. That day I googled NAMI and it was like light bulbs went on. I spend two days reading and downloading information. For the first time we realized our daughter had a mental illness. To this day I am so grateful to the therapist.

I learned about NAMI from a neighborhood newspaper. I went to meetings and became very active. I was on the board, went to several events and went to conferences. From one of the meetings, I heard a speaker from San Fernando Valley Community Mental Health. I went through their two year paraprofessional training program. I became a mental health counselor. I also took NAMI's Family to Family classes.

How long did it take you from the time you heard about the organization to the time you made contact or got involved?

Within days of learning about NAMI, I placed phone calls to a number of affiliates trying to locate a Family to Family class. I left a number of messages but only heard back from one. Though outside our area, we were invited to participate in a class beginning within six weeks. And then, within a couple of weeks, as good fortune would have it, we received a call from our local affiliate and we were able to register for the West Valley class which was twenty five miles closer. All told it was approximately four weeks from the time we placed the calls to the time our Family to Family class began. This association with NAMI began our journey of education, hope, participation in the affiliate and advocacy. Thank you, thank you NAMI SFV!

What's the most important thing that you've learned from organizations like NAMI or have gotten from them?

Practically all that I know about mental illness has come from NAMI. Our local chapter has a publication that they put out every two months which is a treasure trove of useful telephone numbers and resources. They also have books and videos that you can borrow and I think I borrowed all of them at the beginning. I can't speak too highly of those dedicated souls that run the meeting, organize the speakers and provide the resources, all the while dealing with their own family member's illness. They deserve only the very highest praise.

I think if I had to pick one thing from all I've mentioned above as the most important thing I've gotten from NAMI it is that we shouldn't blame ourselves for our family member's illness and that we should try to enjoy the moment. That's what we as a family are trying to do.

My membership and involvement with NAMI has been a tremendous source of knowledge and growth. Speaker meetings, Family to Family classes, conferences, and most important the network of NAMI members are invaluable.. I also occasionally schedule therapy sessions for myself when I am at a loss and need insight into how to handle new situations as they arise.

What other resources besides NAMI been helpful?

NAMI has been my primary volunteer source of advocacy. I am also active in the educational programs of the affiliate, and am involved in regular meetings with a 12-step program. I have been involved with AA with my daughter, attending many meeting with her, and giving her birthday cakes for her sixteenth and eighteenth years of sobriety.

I see many similarities with all of these programs and organizations that are grass roots-based and self-supporting. I am glad to be a part of it all as a family member and a human being who has a less-than-perfect life. I have seen that out of the turmoil of imperfection comes understanding. Understanding is the groundwork for developing patience that is the forerunner of a happy life. Each day I grow a little more, and get a little more happiness.

Have organized programs (AA, NA, other recovery programs) been available and have they worked for you?

When I got sober in 1996 at the age of twenty-six, I thought I was so young and that my life was over after I was told I could not drink—otherwise I would die. I was drawn to AA because a psychiatrist had told me he thought I had a problem staying sober. I knew I was an alcoholic but wanted an easier and safer way to drink. You know, one where I could drink like a lady and not make a fool out of myself. I wanted to get away from the falling-down-drunk stereotype that I had become. But I found out that if I wanted to get sober, I had to do it without ANY alcohol.

I gradually began to tune in at meetings, fighting the urge to drink whenever anything good, bad or indifferent happened. I found a sponsor after two years of being sober but not working the steps. It was all done by white-knuckling it and with prayer. After working a few of the steps, I knew I had to change my "higher power" to God because my 'higher power' had been a literal doorknob. (I hadn't known what to believe, so I had made my higher power a door knob.) I knew in my heart that I had to surrender my life and my will over to the care of God, and I could no longer use the doorknob as my god.

Several more years went by and I discovered a program called "Celebrate Recovery." I began going to meetings and found it exhilarating. I was with other women with problems, with hurts, hang-ups and habits, and I could discuss them openly and spiritually. I found that God really has the power to change us, if we let Him. I found this program to be more giving than AA programs, with far more fellowship. There is love and honesty and loyalty that not all AA groups can proclaim. I am not knocking AA. It got me sober and I am forever grateful to AA for being there when I needed it, but Celebrate Recovery applies Bible scripture, principles and beliefs. It is what I could call 'a heavenly group'. I recommend it to anyone who has issues and a desire to change, using what God gave us—the Bible. For that reason I believe that Celebrate Recovery works best for me.

How do you deal with self-pity?

I found myself talking of nothing but my son's illness; at work, with friends, with family, with neighbors. With each setback, I was devastated, with each step forward, I was elated. And yes, I was angry with him, or angry with his illness. How could this happen to him? ...to us? At times my anger at the unfairness of his illness was unbearable. I felt compelled to tell everyone around me everything about my suffering and pain, my disappointment and distress. It seemed to make it better to hear people tell me, "Oh, it sounds so awful, I am so sorry." It didn't really make it better.

Being an object of pity did not serve any productive purpose. It was just a temporary selfish salve. I could say to myself, 'see, it IS as bad as I thought it was.' But, even though it is very normal to need to talk about our problems and I am fortunate to have been able to open up and talk freely about my concerns, I was not able to pinpoint to whom or when I should talk about my son's illness. Anyone who would listen, or pretend to listen, was a target for more and more updates on my pain. I became more and more isolated. No one really knew what to say to me. No one had any answer.

I realized I was becoming boring, weird, left out of things. Some of my friends stopped contacting me. Others reached out less frequently. Mental illness can isolate us because of the demands of managing day to day life, but my obsessive chattering about my son's illness was making people tune me out.

Fortunately, I found NAMI. I was comforted to be able to funnel the talk about my son's illness to the community of support I found in NAMI. Surrounded by people who had experienced similar challenges, I was able to move through my own chatter and finally came to a point where I didn't need to talk about it all of the time. Finally, I could answer an innocent, "So, how's your son?" with simply "Good...not so good...

better...okay;" instead of a full run-down of the horrors and heartbreaks of seeing our dreams for him disappear again and again.

The habit of self-pity is a hard one to break, but I found that if I focused on helping others, I had less time to suffer. I became an active NAMI volunteer. I learned more about mental illness so I could answer questions with authority instead of purely with emotion, and I realized that my suffering could be put to work to help others. Nothing I do can cure my son. Nothing I do can reclaim the years he has lost to his illness. Now that I have learned more, and now that I make an effort to help others, I can accept the possibility that one day he will recover and have the life that is right for him. And one day, I will too.

How have you managed to become a successful advocate for others living with mental illness?

The first thing I did was to soul search and become involved in spirituality whereby I learned to connect to my higher self. This is an ongoing process and I take classes that enrich my knowledge and keep the healing moving along. The next thing I did was to give back. I became a suicide hotline counselor and helped others in need. This provided tremendous relief and I felt good about helping. I decided to go back to school to work on helping others with addiction issues and am looking for other volunteer situations where I may help others.

Helping others helps me to advocate my growth and hopefully help others who have gone through and are going through the same thing. Being that "someone to talk to," to listen and encourage is the best way I know of how to help others in helping themselves.

How have you found support for yourself? How do you take care of yourself as you deal with these responsibilities?

I had to get hold of myself and get busy. I educated myself about mental disorders. Yoga books, programs, support groups, NAMI.

I go to operas, theater, cinema, re-learned French which I used to speak fluently. Stay in touch with friends, travel, Yoga, long walks. Enjoy the beauty of life and nature. Music. Going to the hairdresser, taking care of yourself and trying not to lose your mind.

I have found a great deal of support from both NAMI and from the Al-Anon Program. My early thought on the problems with my loved one were very simplistic: Simply take your proper medication and don't touch any street drugs. I have found, of course, that mental illnesses are much more complicated and there are so many things that I did not know. There are limitations to what I can expect regarding recovery. Loved ones definitely have limitations to what they can do or handle, depending on the severity of their condition. As I have become more knowledgeable regarding the limitations that my loved one has with rational adult thinking, I have adjusted my expectations.

Al-Anon has helped me deal realistically with the drug and alcohol issues, and helped me to set boundaries that are necessary for me. It has helped me learn better how to take care of myself and not allow my guilt or inability to be effective with my loved one to totally discourage me. NAMI education programs and support have given me many necessary resources and guidance that I would not have known about. Both have been extremely helpful to me.

When I finally did get sober, my life became real. But then I had to experience the pain of going through hurtful experiences that I had once blocked out with drugs and alcohol. I had to deal with life on life's terms and this was all new to me. It was a rough consequence to deal with, but I got my life together.

When are the times that you feel most hopeful?

I feel most hopeful when I know I will not always feel this sad, that it will pass. Trying as hard as possible not to freeze. That has been when I need to go to the hospital for a few days and rest.

WE ARE HERE FOR YOU

We hope you have enjoyed reading this small collection of
Our Wisdom Legacy *Stories*.

There is no fairy tale, happy-ever-after ending. Mental Illness cannot be cured. But Mental Illness *can* be treated and symptoms can be managed. Recovery is possible.

Those who are fortunate to have the support and love of families like the ones who have contributed to this book, and are able to embrace treatment, are the lucky ones.

Studies show that an informed and engaged support system is the most important weapon in the fight for recovery from mental illness. For many of us, finding NAMI-SFV was the beginning of hope and recovery. If you or your loved one suffers from a major mental illness, we can help.

Visit our website
for current classes, programs and services. www.namisfv.org
Contact us for more information 818-994-6747
NAMI SFV 14545 Sherman Circle Van Nuys, CA 91405

GLOSSARY OF TERMS

5150 Hold ... A section of the California Welfare and Institutions Code (specifically, Lanterman–Petris–Short Act or "LPS") which allows a qualified officer or clinician to involuntarily confine a person deemed to have a mental disorder that makes them a danger to self, and/or others and/or gravely disabled.

72 Hour Hold ... A 5150, or 72-hour hold, is a means by which someone who is in serious need of mental health treatment can be transported to a designated psychiatric inpatient facility for evaluation and treatment for up to 72-hours against their will.

AA ... Alcoholics Anonymous: Support for Alcohol Dependency www.aa.org

AB3632 ... Mental Health Services for Special Education Pupils: Ensures that children with disabilities are entitled to a free, appropriate public education in the least restrictive environment.

ADD ... Attention Deficit Disorder: A problem of inattentiveness that interferes with a person's daily functioning.

ADHD ... Attention Deficit Hyperactivity Disorder: A problem of inattentiveness, over-activity, and/or impulsivity that interferes with a person's daily functioning.

BILY ... Because I Love You: Parent and youth support groups for families with trouble children. www.bily.org

Board-and-Care ... Housing that includes room and board, plus supervised care, such as medication supervision.

DSM ... Diagnostic and Statistical Manual of Mental Disorders: Published by the American Psychological Association, provides standard criteria for the classification of mental disorders.

IEP ... Individualized Educational Plan: Utilized in schools to meet educational goals for children with mental or physical disabilities.

LAUSD ... Los Angeles Unified School District www.lausd.net

NA ... Narcotics Anonymous: Support for Drug Dependency www.na.org

OCD ... Obsessive Compulsive Disorder: An anxiety disorder characterized by recurrent, unwanted thoughts and/or repetitive behaviors.

OCPD ... Obsessive Compulsive Paranoid Disorder: An anxiety disorder characterized by recurrent, unwanted thoughts, fear or mistrust of others or situations.

PTSD ... Post Traumatic Stress Disorder: An anxiety disorder that can occur following witnessing or experiencing a traumatic event.

SAS ... Survivors After Suicide: An eight-week support group for family members of suicide victims.

SRO ... Single Room Occupancy. Hotel, rooming house, or hotel-like housing, sometimes provided to homeless individuals through subsidized government or non-profit programs.

SSDI ... Social Security Disability Insurance (paid to individuals who qualify, who have worked or are the qualifying survivor of someone who worked, whose disability makes it impossible for them to work)

SSI ... Social Security Insurance (paid to individuals who qualify, who have never worked, whose disability makes it impossible for them to work)

Al Anon ... Support groups and meetings for friends and family members of people with alcohol dependency. www.al-anon.alateen.org

Anti-depressant ... A medication used for the treatment of depression which works to balance natural brain chemicals, or neurotransmitters, such as serotonin, norepinephrine, and dopamine.

Anti-Psychotic ... A medication used for the treatment of schizophrenia or schizophrenia-related disorders.

Bipolar Disorder ... Formerly known as Manic-Depression. A mood disorder in which a person experiences swings of extreme high and extreme low moods.

Borderline Personality Disorder ... A mental illness characterized by pervasive instability in moods, interpersonal relationships, self-image, and behavior.

Co-Occurring Disorder ... When two disorders occur simultaneously in the same person; for example, mental illness and substance abuse.

Delusion ... A persistent belief in something that is clearly untrue.

Diagnosis ... The identification of the underlying nature or cause of something, such as symptoms of mental illness.

Dual Diagnosis ... A diagnosis made when a person has both a mental illness and a drug or alcohol addiction.

Family to Family ... A NAMI signature twelve-week program offered free to families of individuals with mental illness.

LEAP ... "Listen-Empathize-Agree-Partner" is a communication technique developed by Dr. Xavier Amador in his book "*I am Not Sick I Do Not Need Help*" www.leapinstitute.org

Major Depression ... A mental illness in which a person experiences persistent sadness, feelings of hopelessness, loss of interest in daily activities.

Medi-Cal ... California Medicaid program serving low-income families, seniors, persons with disabilities, children in foster care, pregnant women, and certain low-income adults.

Meds ... Medications

Mental Illness, Severe Mental Illness ... Described by the DSM, diagnosis of a brain disorder that interferes with day to day functioning and can include symptoms such as delusions, psychosis, paranoia, thought and mood disorders.

NAMI ... National Alliance on Mental Illness, support for individuals and family members living with mental illness. www.nami.org

NAMI SFV ... National Alliance on Mental Illness, San Fernando Valley. Los Angeles area affiliate of NAMI, serving San Fernando and Santa Clarita Valleys. www.namisfv.org

Paranoia ... An extreme or irrational fear or distrust of others.

Recovery ... A personal process where a person begins to combat and overcome the difficulties presented by a disorder.

Schizophrenia ... A severe, often debilitating mental illness which interferes with a person's ability to think clearly, manage emotions, make decisions, relate to others.

Schizoaffective Disorder ... A mental illness characterized by a combination of schizophrenic and mood disorder symptoms.

Social Phobia / Social Anxiety Disorder ... A disorder characterized by intense fear of social situations.

Suicide ... The intentional taking of one's own life usually out of despair or troubles attributed to a mental illness.

Wisdom Legacy ... an organization dedicated to gathering stories from various life experiences to inform and enlighten others. This book was created through a collaboration between NAMI SFV and Wisdom Legacy. **www.WisdomLegacy.org**

READING LIST

NAMI SFV members have compiled a reading list of books helpful to understanding and living with mental illness. See the full list on our website www.namisfv.org

An informed and engaged support system of family and friends are among the most effective tools in the fight for recovery from severe mental illness. Attend free NAMI classes, programs and support groups in your area, share this book with others who may benefit from it, and continue your reading with these and other books.

- *"72 Hour Hold"*
  Bebe Moore Campbell

- *"An Unquiet Mind: A Memoir of Moods and Madness"*
  Kay Redfield Jamison

- *"Brain Lock: Free Yourself from Obsessive-Compulsive Behavior"*
  Jeffrey M. Schwartz and Beverly Beyette

- *"I Am Not Sick, I Don't Need Help"*
  Xavier Francisco Amador

- *"His Bright Light"*
  Danielle Steel

- *"Laughter Therapy: How to Laugh About Everything in Your Life That Isn't Really Funny"*
  Annette Gooheart

- *"Potatoes Not Prozac: Solutions for Sugar Sensitivity"*
  Kathleen DesMaisons

- *"The Center Cannot Hold"*
  Elyn R. Saks

INDEX OF QUESTIONS

INDEX OF QUESTIONS

ORDER BOOKS TO SHARE

We encourage you to share this book with friends and family.

You may order e-book version online or order printed book by mail.

To order additional printed copies by mail:

Simply complete the enclosed order form at the back of this book and send it to us with your payment.

All proceeds from the sale of this book support NAMI SFV programs and services to our community, to you, and to your loved ones living with severe mental illness.

ORDER FORM

Please send **Our Stories,** *Things We Know Now We Wish We Knew Then,* NAMI SFV Wisdom Legacy Book @ 9.95 (suggested donation) each plus shipping and handling to:

NAME _____

ADDRESS _____

CITY, STATE, ZIP _____

TELEPHONE(__) _____

EMAIL _____

o I would like _____ books (*) x $13.85

Amount enclosed .... $ _____

o I would like to become a NAMI SFV Member to receive NAMI Newsletter and invitations to NAMI events and conferences. Membership fee enclosed <u>$35.00</u>

Total Amount Enclosed .... $ _____

(*)**Our Stories** Wisdom Legacy Book suggested donation $9.95

Shipping/Handling $3.90

Total $13.85

NAMI SFV is a non-profit charitable organization.

Tax ID # 95-3952653.

All donations are tax deductible as allowed by law.

Please allow 4 weeks for delivery.

Mail this order form with payment (check or money order) to:

NAMI SFV

Our Stories / Wisdom Legacy Book Order

14545 Sherman Circle

Van Nuys, CA 91405

www.namisfv.org

ABOUT THE AUTHORS
ACKNOWLEDGMENTS

Editorial Team

Our Editorial Team gathered, guided, prodded, and polished the work.
We appreciate their dedication and offer heartfelt thanks to:

Lorna Boyd

Rita Keeley Brown

Lynn Conrad

Valeria Reyes

Julia Robinson Shimizu

Cover Design

Ichiro Shimizu

Authors

This book was created with the lived experience and wisdom of
NAMI SFV members. We are grateful to all
who contributed stories.

Thank you.

www.ingramcontent.com/pod-product-compliance
Lightning Source LLC
Chambersburg PA
CBHW060303290526
45789CB00001B/392